# TWISTED GENIUS

# MDC BROOKLYN

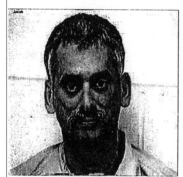

Last Name
## Jacob

First Name
## Craig

Middle Name
## Barry

Date of Photo
## 12/01/1994

A-HLD

REG #:
## 97763-024

W M O  02/03/1953  HT/509  WT/160  HR/GY  EY/BN                    12/01/1994

# twisted genius

**CONFESSIONS OF A $10 MILLION SCAM MAN**

# by Craig Jacob

**AS TOLD TO PHIL BERGER**

FOUR WALLS EIGHT WINDOWS

New York

Published in the United States by:
FOUR WALLS EIGHT WINDOWS
39 West 14th Street, room 503
New York, N.Y., 10011

U.K. offices:
Four Walls Eight Windows/Turnaround
27 Horsell Road
London, N51 XL, England

First printing September 1995.

Library of Congress Cataloging-in-Publication Data:
Jacob, Craig, 1953 -
Twisted genius: confessions of a $10 million scam man /
by Craig Jacob with Phil Berger.
p.    cm.
ISBN: 1-56858-044-4
1. Jacob, Craig, 1953--  . 2. Swindlers and swindling—United States—Case Studies.
I. Berger, Phil. II. Title.
HV6695.J33A3 1995
364.1'63—dc20          95-13291
                    CIP
Text design by LaBreacht Design.

10 9 8 7 6 5 4 3 2 1

Printed in the United States

# Some names have been changed

to protect the innocent

and not-so-innocent.

In certain instances,

banks and other business entities

have been disguised.

# CHAPTER 1

# You look at me and figure:

just another guy, a face in the crowd. It's always been that way. I never was the sort to attract notice. As a kid, I wasn't a charmer or particularly handsome; I didn't have a talent that would make friends and influence people. No. You're talking about a guy who was a "C" student, a benchwarmer on the soccer team. You're talking about a quiet, nondescript fella. A nobody.

At least it looked that way on the surface, I guess. But the truth is that from the time I was a kid I was, no point being modest, a lopsided genius. Like Dustin Hoffman's *Rain Man*, I had a knack. I could look at the everyday routines of commerce and, like-that, know how to exploit them. A scam man's vision for the dishonest buck is what it amounted to. And with that ability I could, and did, screw the system.

I added it up once. Ten million dollars, give or take a few bucks, it came to. And the schemes I concocted to get it were unending. For nearly twenty years I played the biggest institutions for chumps—airlines, banks, casinos, newspapers, credit card companies, Western Union, the phone company, department stores and manufacturers. And never was any element of coercion involved. I mean, no guns, no threats. With con, with guile, sometimes with sheer balls, I took money from these bastions of financial stability. Some of them actually had to change their procedures after I got through with them.

Like the *New York Times*. I was eighteen years old then and about to be expelled from high school for cutting classes in my senior year. My agenda was to bolt school at midday every day so as not to miss the action at Aqueduct, Belmont or Monmouth Park. See, I was a compulsive gambler and, like any such individual, was always in a financial pinch. So, like they say, I got my job through the *New York Times*.

This was back in the days when the *Times* ran its obits with the street addresses of the deceased, a practice followed by newspapers around the country. It was a policy made to order for the plan I put together.

I set up a business, New York Collector Service, with an office in Manhattan and about a dozen people working for me. We had a post office box and an answering service. We bought papers from major cities in the country and would compile our list of names and addresses from those obits.

Then we would generate bills as though we were the collection agency for certain prominent department stores— Macy's, Gimbels, Mays. Each bill was for around one hundred eighty or one hundred ninety dollars and was sent to the address listed in the obit. In the confusion surrounding death, I figured our bill would look as valid as any other and had a real shot at being paid.

We worked on volume. Maybe one of every fifty billings would bring a response, but that was more than enough to make this a very lucrative operation. In nine months, New York Collector grossed more than a hundred thousand dollars. The money would end up being mailed to our post office box by somebody representing the estate—a lawyer, spouse or relative of the deceased. When I'd go to the post office to pick up the money, it would be in large canvas sacks. I'd put the contents in a suitcase, sort out the checks back at the office and convert them to cash.

Picture it. Eighteen years old, and earning the kind of money that men twice my age would envy. I didn't horde it, though—I can tell you that. I was throwing parties at the office, treating my employees to Broadway shows and ballgames. But toward the end of those nine months letters began showing up from the Better Business Bureau because, I guess, folks who somehow doped out that they'd been conned began to complain.

One day, when I walked in to the post office and asked for New York Collector's mail, the woman at the counter told me I'd have to go to the second floor to see the postal inspector before she could give me it. No problem, I told her, and I calmly turned to go. Out the door and onto the street I went, leaving that postal inspector and New York Collector forever behind me. And soon after, the *New York Times* stopped using the addresses of our most prominent dead in their daily obituaries.

# While New York Collector

was a pretty fair scam, I don't want to leave the impression that I was particularly smooth, or sophisticated, in those days. 'Cause I wasn't. Mostly I just passed bad checks, or wrote checks on my mother's accounts that she never knew about. Never knew because when the mail came I'd remove my checks from the monthly statement and reseal the envelope. She wasn't too thorough a recordkeeper, so if there was a deficit she'd simply cover it at the bank without bothering to find out why there was a problem to begin with.

I got caught plenty in those days, but time and again the courts would let me off with probation and a warning not to do it again. But when you're a degenerate gambler, restraint is no part of the deal. So when my gambling debts got me in a hole again....boom—I'd figure another way to get the money and be back at it again.

That need to be in action was forged early on. I suspect I was most influenced by my grandfather, Bert Barnett. He did things his way and never let sentiment interfere with his getting ahead. Grandpa never wanted to be a wage slave to another man, and never was. Through ingenuity and that cold wit for business, he made himself the big man I admired as a boy and, maybe subconsciously, emulated as an adult. I liked the way he carried big wads of hundred-dollar bills in his pockets and the way he paid for everything in cash. Strictly cash.

My grandfather had come to the States from England when he was in his early twenties. His father had owned a lumber yard over there, and one of his employees was Harry Houdini. Houdini's job was to move lumber about the yard, and part of Bert's job was to wake Houdini every morning. Apparently, Houdini was a heavy sleeper.

When Bert married my grandmother, Celia, she was working for Purolator (which made oil filters) in Elizabeth, New Jersey. He used the money she earned to start his own business. What he did was buy a lot of small appliances, paying a thousand dollars to wholesalers in New York for stuff like irons, washboards, toasters and radios.

Then, say he'd paid a dollar per iron, he'd turn around and sell that iron in poor neighborhoods for a dollar down and twenty-five cents a week. He would never tell the customers what the actual cost was. And the way the paper they signed read was that the poor shnook paid until Grandpa said he could stop...which amounted to the day the guy was dead. I think the wording in the contract was something like, "We will advise you when the item is paid in full." By that system, he might end up with a hundred, hundred fifty dollars for a one-dollar iron if the customer kept up his payments over the years.

Now, while fifty percent of those poor people would make the down payment and skip out—not necessarily to beat Grandpa...they were poor and tended to move around a lot—the other fifty percent he dunned for their weekly payment. At first he had his son Irwin, and a few other collectors, going door to door in their cars. But after a customer poked Irwin in the nose, Grandpa bought Wells Fargo-style vans and, when the collectors came to the door, they had German shepherds with them.

I'd be there in the office when the collectors showed up and threw paper bags filled with money on my grandfather's desk. Cash would also be sent through the mail. Once in a while, when nobody was looking I'd dip into those bags and filch fifty or sixty dollars. I was ten years old, and would use the money to buy baseball cards and postage stamps that I traded with other kids.

These thefts left Grandpa puzzled.

"It's off," he'd tell his collectors, in a tone that indicated he believed they were cheating him.

Grandpa did so well in the 1950s that he moved from Newark to Hillside, New Jersey, bought a house for Celia and him, and gave the realtor the asking price of twenty-six thousand dollars in one lump sum, all cash. He then gave my mother twenty-six thousand dollars in cash to buy the house next door to him. She took the money but made the minimum down payment for the house and stuck the rest in her account.

I overheard her telling my grandparents: "I want my husband to work and pay a mortgage like everybody else. I'm not putting him on Easy Street."

Anyway. Once he got to Hillside, Grandpa ordered a trailerload of furniture from a factory in North Carolina—all living-room sets. He unloaded the truck and filled the entire basement of his home and his garage with the furniture. And then he had Irwin and the other workers go back to the poor neighborhoods with pictures of the furniture sets, soliciting the same people who had bought the irons and toasters.

Grandpa had paid one hundred twenty-five dollars per living-room set and now he charged one hundred twenty-five dollars down and twelve dollars a week...for as long as he could get it. And he did get it, by garnisheeing salaries without a pang of conscience.

However, he went to court one time too many, suing a fella who brought his contract and then explained to the judge about the exorbitant amount he had paid for a one-dollar iron. Grandpa was chastized by the court and told that what he was doing was illegal. No big thing. Grandpa immediately changed his policy. That one hundred twenty-five dollar living-room set now cost you one hundred twenty-five dollars  down and twelve dollars a week for the next one hundred fifty weeks. And that was perfectly legal and perfectly profitable.

I spent a lot of time with Grandpa, and admired the way he operated. As a kid, I'd say to myself: "That's the way I want to be. Rolls of one-hundred-dollar bills in my pocket and never have to work for anybody."

Anyway. I grew up in Hillside, New Jersey, in a middle-class neighborhood not far from where the truly rich lived in mansions. From the age of twelve, I was a hardcore card player, sitting across the table from boys my age who came from those wealthy families. We played a regular weekly game, frequently at Kenny Rickel's house. Rickel's father owned a lumber and home appliance business and advertised regularly on television. Old man Rickels got a kick out of seeing his kid playing poker, or black jack, or acey deucey, and would pace up and back, bankrolling his son with fresh capital from the wad of bills he'd carry.

Though we were only twelve, the stakes were hardly penny-ante. A player could easily drop five hundred to one thousand dollars a night. I was at a disadvantage in that respect. Where the other kids came to the table with five hundred dollars, or better, I'd walk in with only one hundred dollars. Yet I was no pigeon for these rich boys. I won my share, and did it the old-fashioned way. I cheated.

One day, when we were playing next door to Rickel's, at Ross Stein's house, I saw a spare set of keys. Knowing the Steins would be away the next week, I stole the keys and the following day, while a friend of mine played lookout, let myself in. In that weekly game of ours, we used a brand of cards called Bicycle. The cards were kept in a drawer in the Stein's rec room. I found two boxes—a total of twenty-four decks. I stole those cards and drove across the river to New York City.

I went straight to a place on 42nd Street that sold Bicycle cards that were sealed but marked. Twenty-four marked decks for a total of two hundred dollars. Back in Hillside, I returned to the Steins' house and switched their decks for mine. No surprise, I began to have some very profitable nights at the card table. For six months I won about a thousand dollars a week.

On days when there was no card game, I'd go to the race track, sometimes even travelling up to Vermont because none of the tracks in the metropolitan New York area were open on Sunday. But in Green Mountain, Vermont, the horses ran on Sundays. Between the race track and the occasional trip to Las Vegas, whatever money I made with my rigged decks was quickly gone.

Vegas was my Disneyland. I loved the excitement, and the fact that you could gamble around the clock there. In real life, there were always limits. When our card game, for instance, would begin to wind down, I'd get very uneasy—a low-grade anxiety. I never wanted the action to stop. For me, gambling was a high that kept me far removed from the hum-drum world.

In spite of my youth, I was able to gamble with impunity in Las Vegas. Part of that had to do with the mustache I had, which made me look older than the minimum age, which was eighteen. The only time I had a problem was at the Riviera Hotel and Casino. I was sixteen on a night I won seven thousand dollars there shooting craps. Casino security followed me to my room and demanded to see ID. When they realized I was underage, they told me: "Pack up, kid, and be out of here by midnight." I was, proceeding across the street to the Stardust, where I continued to win. It was one of the few times I went home with money in my pocket.

As a rule I usually lost my money. Which put me in this quandary: I couldn't stand being out of action merely for lack of funds. So I began tapping into money that had been placed in bank accounts for me after my bar mitzvah. The haul from my bar mitzvah had amounted to fifty grand, in cash, stock and bonds. Eventually, my parents noticed the money had disappeared and became convinced I was using it to buy drugs. But drugs held no interest for me in those days. I was crazy to gamble.

After I went through the bar mitzvah money, I began operating as a bookie in high school. My betting line came from the *Newark Star-Ledger,* enabling me to make book on baseball, football and the horses. I got a big kick out of handling all that action. In a weird way it compounded the pleasure of gambling. For instance, guys usually bet heavily on, say, two horses per race, which meant I had all the other horses. I liked that feeling of eight or nine horses going for me. And I liked the money I made—about eight hundred dollars a week.

One day, acting on an anonymous tip, the Hillside police entered the school and confiscated the records of my book-making operation from my locker. The cops called my father and told him: "If you get the kid to cease and desist, we won't arrest him. We know he's taking a college prep course and don't want to ruin his life."

So I stopped taking the action of other students. But it hardly deterred my need to gamble. A year after I'd made that seven-thousand-dollar score in Vegas, I hit it bigger, a lot bigger. I won one hundred twelve thousand dollars playing craps. I'd gone out there with a girlfriend whose parents thought we were staying the weekend at a beach house in Bradley Beach, New Jersey. Hot as I was with the dice, I didn't want to leave Vegas. But we had our high-school prom to go to. So reluctantly I let myself be persuaded to catch the flight back. Stuffed the money into a shoulder bag and, when I made it back home, threw thirty thou into the same bank that held the bar mitzvah account with the fifty grand that I'd gone through. The rest was gambling money. I used it day and night to gamble...until it was gone. That didn't stop me. I gambled without letup. By now I was going to extremes to get money to do it. I persuaded a girlfriend who was a supermarket cashier to be my accomplice in robbing her Pathmark. I was broke again, and so was she—I'd used her money to gamble with and blown it. She told me the nightly cash pickups were made at 9 P.M. and in her register there would be at least five grand. I showed up at 8:45 and, as prearranged, she had all the money in a paper bag under the counter. She threw my groceries on top and waited until I was just about to my car before yelling she'd been robbed.

Too late. I was long gone with the five grand before the Hillside police showed up, looking for a robber she described as a tall black man. Given that I am an average-sized white man, this constituted a rather diversionary description and one that did not withstand the polygraph test her Pathmark bosses gave her. She was fired. To add insult to injury, I then went out and squandered the five grand gambling.

No matter. I still lived in style. Somehow or other, I'd come up with the money...or figure a way to outwit the system. Take the rental cars I drove for practically nothing. In those days, your rental car companies weren't yet computerized the way they are today. That meant the rental clerks would fill out the forms by hand. That meant I could screw the system.

What I would do was rent a car from National, Hertz or Avis on, say, March first...and then return it on the first day of the next month. If I rented it from Newark Airport, I'd return it to LaGuardia Airport. But when I'd return the form, I'd alter the rental date so that instead of reading that I'd rented it March 1, it would now read "March 31."

For a month's rental of a late-model car, I'd pay the grand sum of fourteen dollars or so. Then I'd rent my next car that day from John F. Kennedy Airport and return it to a down-town Manhattan outlet a month later. And alter the date again when I returned it.

The only other thing was to lie about the mileage on the car. Since the rental car employees rarely checked out the mileage you claimed, it wasn't hard to get away with driving six hundred miles for what appeared to be a one-day rental.

Lots of times I drove those cars into the city. I liked the excitement of New York. There was always something going on there. Some of it was a little bent. Like the three-card monte games.

If you're not familiar with three-card monte, let me explain what it involves. Usually, there's a guy standing over a large carton that serves as a table, and he's manipulating three cards that are facedown—moving them manually along the table. Two of the cards are black—clubs or spades. The other is red—hearts or diamonds. As he's moving the cards, he's spieling: "Where's the red? Find the red."

After he's finished moving the cards around, you put your money down and bet on which facedown card is the red. And usually you lose your dough 'cause these guys are very slick.

But I was a high-school kid and fascinated. I watched and watched and believed he couldn't beat me. So I bet a ten on the red and lost. And twice more dropped a ten-dollar bill chasing that elusive red card.

I remember walking away disappointed and pissed. And determined to get even.

There was a magic shop not far from that Times Square three-card monte. The store sold invisible-ink tricks. The kits came with these goofy-looking glasses, like 3-D glasses, that enabled you to see the yellow-stained invisible ink. Without the glasses, you saw nothing.

I bought the invisible ink and glases, and back to the three-card monte game I went.

You were supposed to dip a pen into this tiny bottle of fluid, but I just applied the bottle to my thumb and waited until a big pot developed—several people throwing down money to chase the red card and none of them winning.

Well, I pretended to be skeptical and grabbed the red card while the dealer protested: "Hey. Whatcha doin', man?"

"Just wanted to make sure there wasn't a black card underneath it."

"Hey, man. We don't cheat. And don't touch the damn cards."

Too late. I'd gotten my thumbprint on the back of the red card and now could read the red whenever the cards were shifted around. I won a few—ten dollars here, twenty dollars there. And had worked my way up to one hundred dollars. That's when I decided to bet the whole thing...the one hundred dollars. And when I guessed the red again, that's when one of the dealer's accomplices hollered: "Cops!" And they bolted to avoid paying me. At least I was quick enough to grab my hundred before they got away.

Of course, there were no cops anywhere in sight.

In those days I was A.W.O.L. from classes so often that by the time I was a senior, school authorities had no choice: they expelled me. I left New Jersey for Miami Beach, staying at my grandmother's condo while working as a hotel parking attendant. In a month there, I earned enough in tips and wages to buy a used Chevy so I could travel to the dog races and jai alai.

The Bahamas were not far from Miami and I'd never been to the casinos there. I hit on a scheme to raise the price of the airfare there—plus additional capital that would allow me to gamble in comfort. What I did was stop in at various branches of a local department store called "Jefferson's," and buy merchandise for amounts ranging between one hundred and two hundred dollars. I paid for the goods with checks drawn on an account of mine that had no money it. That day, or the next, I would return the merchandise to Jefferson's for a cash refund. In the meantime, I was also cashing fifty-dollar checks from the same worthless account at half-a-dozen J. C. Penney stores. Within two days I'd put together a war chest of a thousand dollars for the trip.

It was only a matter of time before the courts decided enough was enough and made me do time. For a two-hundred-dollar bum check I was sent to a youth facility in Ashland, Kentucky. It was 1972, and I was nineteen years old.

# Ashland was scary.

In my two weeks in orientation there, I saw an inmate stabbed for cutting ahead in line in the dining hall and another guy doused with gasoline and lit on fire on the baseball field. I wanted out of there.

In a copy of the *Village Voice* that was sent to me, I read about a youth facility in Morgantown, West Virginia. The article made the place out as a sort of correctional paradise. Pictures of women in miniskirted uniforms. Recreational facilities. Unbelievable. I phoned my parents and told them get me Morgantown, and quick. Lord knows, I fit the criteria—first offender, nonviolent. My mother, Jeanne, sent a telegram to Richard Nixon. Four days later, I was picked up by a marshall and shipped to Morgantown, at just about the time Watergate was blowing Nixon out of the White House.

In Morgantown, there were no fences, and each inmate had his own room. There was a gym, an indoor swimming pool, a fishing pond, miniature golf, park benches all over. Every Friday and Saturday night, dances were held and girls from other institutions were bussed in to even out the social disparity at Morgantown—three hundred men, one hundred women. Wednesdays was pizza party night—pizza served from eight to eleven, bring your own girlfriend.

Mine was Helen, a pretty blonde with a great figure. She'd been busted for dealing drugs back in Jacksonville, Florida. Small-time stuff, really. I'd see her evenings. Days, I had a prison job as a teacher's aide from 8 A.M. to 11 A.M., tutoring math, reading, everything. Afternoons I was matriculating at the University of West Virginia, even though I'd never graduated high school. What the hell, I told them I had and nobody bothered to check.

I'd get back from the university late afternoon and hang out with Helen until curfew, which was 9 P.M. Sexual relations were tabu. If you got caught, you got in trouble. But for most of us, it didn't discourage our trying anyway. There were lots of sexy women, plenty of them hookers in civilian life who didn't mind giving it away while doing time. In fact, before I'd met Helen, I'd made love to a seventeen-year-old girl named Susan Case, who was in for dealing drugs too.

As part of my rehabilitation, I was let out occasionally to go to meetings of Gamblers Anonymous in Youngstown, Ohio. My second time out, I detoured to the Meadows, a race track in Pittsburgh. I won three hundred dollars betting the trotters and hid the money in my shoes. When they searched me back at Morgantown, they found the money and tossed me in the segregation unit.

Some punishment. The segregation unit was twenty-four rooms, co-ed, with no staff around. So it was all sex. While I was there it was twenty girls and three guys, and girls just blatantly taking their clothes off and carrying on.

Helen had been in the segregation unit for infractions of her own. So she knew what went on there, and kept sending me threatening notes about what she'd do to me if I touched another woman. Helen was a bit strange about men. I think she'd been abused when she was young. When other men approached her she'd stiffen, as though she was afraid of them. For some reason, she wasn't that way with me. Maybe because I was real low-key. I don't know. Tell you the truth, I never was all that smart about women.

Anyway. I kind of dug Helen and had no intention of cheating on her in the segregation unit. But one afternoon there, as I was shooting pool with a girl named Lacey—long legs and red hair down to her waist—she rubbed up against me and grabbed my dick and said, "I wanna fuck you, Jake."

Two minutes later, she got her wish.

# I did two years

in Morgantown and wasn't back home in Jersey for long when I got a call from Susan Case, the first girl I'd slept with at Morgantown.

She had been transferred to another prison and, about to be released, asked if I would pick her up.

I caught a plane out of Newark, to Roanoke, Virginia—the closest commercial destination to Alderson Federal Institute for Women. There I picked up Susan who, like Helen, was a blonde with a great figure. She was also bisexual. At Morgantown, she had fooled around with other women and hadn't been shy about telling me. We made love at a motel near the Roanoke airport, drove north to New Jersey and spent a few days together. We had fun but really didn't have the sort of chemistry I had with Helen. I bought Susan an airline ticket from Newark to her hometown of Memphis...and that was the last I saw of her.

I got a job with a company in Brooklyn that made envelopes, all kinds of envelopes. I was fascinated by the business, which ran seven days a week, twenty-four hours a day. I worked hard, putting in long hours, and the bosses took a liking to me. In no time, I rose from assistant production manager to shipping manager, my salary jumping from two hundred to five hundred dollars a week. But it wasn't enough to cover my gambling losses.

I figured a way to supplement my income, based on a government contract the company had gotten. That contract was for a wide-ranging order of envelopes for government agencies—for the IRS, the Federal Reserve, the Navy, prisons.

The contract stipulated that only a couple of government agencies would permit the company to use prepaid government postage. Those prepaid labels were sent to me. Part of my job was to make sure that there was postage on all the cartons we shipped to the various government agencies. To cover those costs, I was advanced a thousand dollars a week.

But rather than waste it on postage, I pocketed the money and xeroxed the prepaid labels—made about a thousand of those labels and slapped them on all the cartons. Did it over a period of about four months, earning roughly a thousand dollars a week.

Yet even that extra money wasn't enough to take care of my gambling habit. Eventually I told my bosses I had a job offer for one hundred fifty dollars a week more than they were paying. They told me good luck with the other job. Trouble was there was no other job. I was bluffing. They'd called my bluff. That meant I was out of work.

The loss of that job couldn't have come at a worst time. Helen (my girlfriend from Morgantown) and I were living in Lefrak City in Rego Park in a three hundred dollar a month apartment and, by some quirk, had not been billed our rent for twelve months. Then suddenly a three-thousand-six-hundred-dollar rent bill arrived—twelve months at three hundred dollars per month.

The bill materialized at a time when I was into bookies and loan sharks for ten grand, and owed credit card companies another twenty-five grand. No question about it: We had to steal out in the middle of the night and find a new place to live.

I thumbed through the *New York Times*, looking for an apartment. And found a lot more.

The rental ad read like this:

> "SUTTON PLACE, Apt for sublease, June 1 through Aug 1, two months only, furnished, excel ref only. $1,200 per month plus security. Call Miss Weinstock at (phone number)..."

The scam came to me like a vision. From beginning to end, I instinctively knew what I needed to make it work. First was to get hold of the two thousand four hundred dollars Miss Weinstock wanted up front—a month's rent and a month's security. That money was my ticket to ride, so I borrowed it from a loan shark.

Then I phoned Miss Weinstock to corroborate the details in the ad, to make sure there was nothing omitted that would change the way I would do things. Her emphasis, it turned out, was what I gathered from the ad. She wanted to make sure she was getting a reputable tenant whose credentials would check out. I hung up at that point without giving her my name.

Next I took a cab over to the New York Hilton. In the past I'd had my hair cut at the hotel barber shop, so I knew that there were always conventions going on there. On this afternoon, there was a bankers convention. Perfect. I wore a coat and tie, slipped into the ballroom and mingled. Every once in a while, I would step off to the side to write down potential names. The one I liked best was a "Joe Roberts" from a bank in California. He looked like me and was about my age. I phoned his bank and asked for him. The woman on the other end told me Joe Roberts was out of town on business and not expected back for a while.

"How long?" I asked.

"Oh, probably four to five weeks."

"You're sure?"

"Yes sir."

I walked over to a twenty-four-hour printing shop and had them make me some business cards with Joe Roberts's name and the bank and its address on them. Once I had the card, I called Miss Weinstock and made an appointment to see her.

She was an older woman, in her sixties, who was going to Israel for a couple of months to visit a relative. I got the feeling she was independently wealthy: the place was lavishly furnished and she had a way about her that suggested she had no money problems. None whatsoever.

I brought Helen with me and told her not to say anything, just smile, act nice and pretend to be my wife. I figured it would look better that way than my showing up alone. I walked in with the Joe Roberts business card and some of my own credit cards. But I had no intention of showing her anything other than the business card, although when I opened the wallet I made sure she caught a glimpse of all the credit cards.

As soon as I handed her the bogus business card, she phoned the bank and one-two-three my identity and respectability were established. Yes yes, he works for us, they told her. I gave her the two-thousand-four-hundred-dollar cashier's check. The apartment was mine. Now came the real action.

I phoned the *New York Times* and placed an ad for an apartment to sublet, with the same details that Miss Weinstock had included in her advertisement, except I altered the dates when the apartment would be available, thereby giving me time to run the scam.

"Call Mr. Weinstock," the *Times* ad read, and it gave Miss Weinstock's phone number.

The phone rang without letup. I began scheduling appointments every hour on the hour for the potential sub-lessors. By now I had standard lease forms that I picked up for fifteen-cents per copy from a stationery store in the neighborhood. I had them all filled out except for the signature.

I changed the sublease clause to eight hundred dollars a month to make it seem more attractive and asked for an additional one-thousand-six-hundred-dollar security. I rented the place to sixty-odd people over a three-week period—people ranging from Florida to Boston and one from as far away as Denver. Told them all I was relocating to Philadelphia. Most people gave checks, some gave cash. Figure it out: sixty times two thousand four hundred dollars. That's more than one hundred and twenty thousand dollars.

I put the money in an account I opened in the name of Herbert Weinstock at Chemical Bank, using as ID a Macy's card and a social security card that I found in a closet in Miss Weinstock's place.

One day, three weeks and one hundred twenty thousand dollars into my scam, I got a phone call from a Beverly Cole, one of the select group of sixty I'd sublet the apartment to. She said that she was concerned about how legitimate her sublet was, as four days after she'd signed the lease form, her sister, Fran, had told her she had sublet the same apartment.

It was one of those wild coincidences. But I didn't let it fluster me.

"That's not true," I told Beverly. "Your sister is in 3-C. Across the hall from the apartment I sublet to you. I have two apartments here. Come on over and I'll show you. I don't want you to be the least concerned. If by accident I made a mistake, no problem. I'll correct it. Your sister will get 3-C."

The other sister then called to verify what I'd told Beverly. She was happy and excited to be living across from her sister.

"Come right over," I said. "We'll get this straightened out. I'm terribly sorry to have troubled you."

I left Miss Weinstock's apartment and never went back.

A month later, the *New York Post* headline read: FLIM FLAM MAN RIPS OFF 66 WEALTHY FAMILIES and the front page had a picture of the 59th Street bridge jammed with trailers that the editors said, tongue in cheek, were all bound for the Weinstock apartment.

# Now that I had money,

I cleared my debts with the bookies and credit card companies. Subtract that plus my gambling losses, and I still had sixty to seventy grand left.

I rented an apartment on Columbus Avenue, near Columbia University, and began working for a linen company that sold fancy towels to bath shops and upscale department stores. When one of the salesmen who worked Virginia and North Carolina became sick and retired, I asked for and got his job.

As these things went, it was a giant step up. He had been grossing one hundred and fifty thousand dollars a year, and I'd been making maybe a quarter of that. So it was better money and weekends free to run to Las Vegas and gamble.

I moved to Norfolk, Virginia, and with Helen settled into a house I bought. I worked hard as a salesman and was constantly traveling. There was very little gambling in the area. To get action I would fly to Vegas on weekends.

In eleven months working my territory, I earned a little more than eighty thousand dollars. The problem was I'd blown a hundred thousand dollars gambling. I was in debt again, owing my parents, friends, casinos, bookies and loan sharks. Even though I was tapped out, I flew to Vegas one weekend and signed for a ten-thousand-dollar marker with practically no money to cover it in my bank account back in Virginia.

It took me about eight hours to blow the ten grand and then I returned to Norfolk. Sales had been good. I expected a sizeable commission check at the end of the month. My credibility with the United Virginia Bank was good. I had never overdrawn my savings account. My checking plus account held fifteen hundred dollars that I never used. The tellers all knew me because I deposited large monthly paychecks, usually seven to eight thousand dollars. For that community that was big money.

The marker that I signed in Vegas bore my checking account number with United Virginia Bank. At the time that I signed the marker I was fully aware that my bank account balance was only four hundred dollars, but I figured that the marker would be returned to the casino and then the casino would contact me about making good on it. I'd make good and that would be that.

Well, United Virginia Bank did not return the marker to the casino. The bank paid it because I was a good customer. Then they called to say, "Please make a deposit to cover that check."

I called my office in New York and asked for a ten-thousand-dollar advance, but was refused. I thought about flying to Vegas and taking out another ten-thousand-dollar marker to use to pay the bank back. But I figured that that elaborate a plan was not necessary. I figured that since I generated the kind of money I did, I'd be able to talk reasonably to the bank about a solution.

I went in and spoke to one of the bank execs.

"Look, I'm a gambler and I'm a little short right now," I told him. "But by the end of the week I have a ten-thousand-dollar commission check coming. I can give you five of it."

That was five grand against the nine thousand six hundred dollars I owed.

"And the rest of it the following week," I said. "Minus the fifteen hundred dollars in my checking plus, which you can have now."

"We'll see," he said, and when I left he called the cops.

I was arrested. Rather than stand trial, I split and went back to New York, with Helen. I got a job as a dispatcher with a trucking company located in Jersey City, New Jersey, and, on the side, I drove for them. With both jobs, I was making about eight hundred dollars a week. I tried and did cut down my gambling. I wanted to save enough money to open my own business.

To get my nut for that business, I didn't mind working a bit dirty. Here's how that went. Sometimes, when guys loaded trucks, they'd put extra skids on, containing merchandise there was no record of—like, say, forty-thousand-dollars worth of Taster's Choice Coffee. Strange as it sounds, sometimes goods would arrive without corresponding paperwork. A lively opportunity for a fella like me.

I found a guy on Fulton Street in Brooklyn, who would buy illicit goods for his discount store. For a shipment like that I could stick fifteen grand in my pocket.

I worked at the trucking company five months before opening up Worldwide Distribution, a discount store in Long

Island City. I used that name because it was the same one that my wealthy grandfather used for his furniture business. When I applied for loans for the business, I made as though my Worldwide Distribution was his, to give the banks the impression I'd been doing business for twenty-five years or so. That way, the banks would be more amenable to giving me start-up money.

Armed with a hundred-thousand-dollars worth of bank loans, I opened up my store. To supplement my merchandise, I occasionally dealt in "swag," stolen merchandise. Business prospered. I had five employees and a nice routine. Middays I'd empty out the cash register, take the proceeds and head off to the racetrack with it. In the evening, I'd return for a second cash pickup and a night at the trotters.

It was while I was at the track that complications occurred one day. My manager, George, happened to look up as Helen rang up a bottle of perfume on the cash register. By mistake, she hit a price of $2.20 when the actual price was twenty-two dollars. When George pointed out her error, Helen got angry— embarrassed at what she'd done (she was not awfully bright)—and told him he was fired. When I showed up later that day, George was gone and I had to patch together the story of what had happened.

I wasn't happy. I trusted George. He was smart. He knew the business. So long as George was there, I felt comfortable about taking off to watch the ponies. Without George around, I couldn't be sure that things would run as smoothly.

I persuaded George to come back, promising him that Helen would stay away. But she didn't. In spite of my promise to get her a job elsewhere, she took to showing up at the store. One day, I phoned a school crossing guard from the neighborhood and asked her to stop by in her guard uniform. I told her to pretend to be the police and warn Helen she must stay away from the premises.

It worked. She scared Helen into leaving the store, telling her that if she didn't, she would be arrested for trespassing. But Helen was pissed and gave me the silent treatment when I got home later that night.

A few days later, Helen showed up at the store and walked straight to the phone. Picked it up, dialed a number and said, "FBI? I'm calling about Worldwide Discount Store in Long Island City. The owner has stolen merchandise." She hung up and walked out.

We figured she was kidding. But pretty soon suspicious types began nosing around the store. You know, buying a pack of gum and browsing very intensely while pretending not to be. George and I made sure that the goods on the shelf were all clean—no swag.

Soon after, the FBI raided the place. Wild. They came SWAT-team style, with shotguns and loud voices: "Nobody move! You're under arrest for possession of stolen property from an interstate shipment!"

Funny: the customers who happened to be in the store at the time of the bust took the arrival of the FBI as a green light to snatch whatever goods they could and walk out of the store without paying for anything.

Anyway. I was arrested and, as I was led out of the store by the police, I saw the owners of the trucking company, which by now had gone bankrupt, sitting in a car. As I was taken away, they left their car and headed into the store. It later was revealed they marked a number of cases of my merchandise as being stolen. Total bullshit. The store was, by then, clean. But it gave the authorities a case against me and gave the trucking guys a story for their insurance company.

By then, I was living on 62nd Street and First Avenue in a luxury Manhattan building. That night, when Helen came home, the doorman asked her for her key, as I had instructed him to. Then he showed her that her bags were packed and waiting for her. She began crying and called the cops on me. They came up and asked to see the lease to the apartment. When they saw the apartment was in my name, they told Helen she would have to leave. She began bawling again. The cops came back up and asked if I could give her money so she could fly home. I gave them five hundred dollars for her, and figured that was the end of my problems with Helen.

My problems with the law were compounding. As the authorities checked things out, they discovered that I had lied on my loan applications, misrepresenting the number of years that my Worldwide had been in business. That was a federal crime, and a bigger headache for me than the so-called stolen goods in my store. I could see me doing serious time on the federal rap. So I went on the lam again rather than stand trial.

Now began an odyssey that would take me all over the country—Philadelphia, Reno, Los Angeles, San Francisco, Las Vegas, Tampa, Fort Lauderdale, Chicago. Nearly fifteen years in which I kept changing my identity while devising schemes that generated big money, millions of dollars that I'd squander sooner or later on gambling. And that would lead me to improvise still another scam to fill my pockets full again. The never ending cycle.

While it lasted, it was a blast.

# CHAPTER 6

# When the FBI closed my

store, I was damn near broke—down to my last thousand dollars. That thousand bucks didn't even cover a month's rent on my apartment. So I decided to take the money and bet it at the track. Bet the whole thou on a horse.

I'd made up my mind that if the horse won, I'd take the money and start a new life far from the city of my miseries.

If the horse lost, who the hell knew.

Well, as I arrived at the track, I could hear the announcer say: "...Just two minutes until post time, just two minutes."

I never looked at what race I was betting or what horses were in it. I'd decided that whatever the race was I'd bet the number five horse—five was my grandfather's favorite number—and take pot luck.

At the ticket window, I said: "A thousand dollars to win on the number five."

I then walked outside to watch the race. I glanced up at the tote board and saw that I had bet on the seventh race, the feature race, and that I had put my last thousand on an eighteen-to-one horse named Hey Hey JP.

Well, Hey Hey JP broke dead last but as the pack headed for the wire he'd worked his way among the leaders.

"Come on, JP," I screamed, my life seeming to hang in the balance. "Come on."

As the horses charged to the finish line, Hey Hey JP was coming on fast. Very fast.

"Get 'em, JP," I screamed. "Get 'em."

A photo finish was too close to call, requiring the stewards to resolve the matter. I paced back and forth as they conferred. Then, over the loud speaker: "Ladies and gentlemen, after reviewing the photo, we declare Hey Hey JP the winner."

I collected nineteen thousand dollars as an advance on a new life.

The next day, I caught a train to Philadelphia. Got off at 30th Street station. A day later, my second interview, I landed a job at the *Philadelphia Bulletin*, one of the local newspapers. The controller gave me a quick tour of the plant. Back in his office, I was filling out forms when he got a call that required him to leave me alone for a while.

As soon as he walked out of the office, I looked around the room and my eye fixed on a large checkbook ledger and a separate pile of bank statements on a shelf behind his desk. I opened the checkbook, which contained blank checks used by the newspaper. I ripped two pages of checks from the middle of the book. Then I took two canceled checks from one of the statements and noted a balance in the account of ninety-two thousand dollars. I shoved everything in my back pocket and sat down, just as the controller returned to his office.

I worked at the *Bulletin* for two weeks before persuading myself I could not survive on two hundred eighty-nine dollars a week. In my two weeks there, I had lost eleven thousand of my nineteen thousand dollars gambling. So I pulled out the canceled *Bulletin* checks and began practicing the signature on them. It took me an hour to feel comfortable doing it. I signed all six blank checks and headed to a local library.

My intention was to type the checks out to Alan Greenspan. It was under that name I had a bullshit ID card. But on the way to the library I found a Pennsylvania driver's license in the name of Edward Davis in the gutter. The description matched me to a T and Pennsylvania licenses back then did not have photos. This was a better ID for me, I decided. So at the library I typed out the checks to Edward Davis, each one in the amount of ten thousand dollars. I then opened an account at the Girard Bank and Trust, using two hundred dollars in cash to start it.

The next day, in suit and tie I deposited all six checks in six different branches of the Girard Bank. The checks were drawn on the Girard bank and the following day all the funds were available in the account. So I wrote out a withdrawal slip for twenty thousand dollars and noted on the slip that I wanted American Express traveler's checks. To turn a traveler's check into cash at any Las Vegas hotel was as easy as turning casino chips to cash.

Thirty minutes later I did the same at another branch. This time, though, when the teller brought my account up on her computer, she said she'd be right back. As she walked to the back, a bank officer headed for the doors with the keys in his hand. He locked the doors, leaving me as the only customer inside. By now I could see "my" teller had no intention of finishing my transaction. She was in the back, staring at me. I walked over to the bank officer and told him I could wait no longer.

"I've got to be somewhere—I'll take care of this tomorrow," I said, gesturing for him to open the door.

"It'll only be a moment, sir," he said, stalling me.

So I grabbed his keys off his desk and ran for the doors. As I was inserting the key, he came running up and shoved me hard, shoved me right through the plate-glass window, just as a police cruiser pulled up.

I got to my feet, bleeding from the forehead. At the hospital, it took nine stitches to close the wound. When the police brought me in for questioning, they seemed confused about what I'd done and if it was illegal. After all, there was money in the account and I had the ID showing me to be Edward Davis.

But then the cops asked me had I ever been arrested and I told them no.

"You're a liar," the detective shouted. "You know you've been arrested. Who you trying to bullshit?"

"I'm not lying," I said, apprehensively.

At first I was worried that I had climbed into an identity that was going to cause me all kinds of grief because of a sorry and criminal past. But it turned out that Edward Davis had once been arrested for possession of marijuana in high school.

"Oh, that," I said. "They told me they'd wipe it from my record if I stayed clean for a year. That's penny-ante shit."

That seemed to cool them out. Whatever. I was held overnight, and the next day met with a pre-bail investigator, who asked me all kinds of questions. Where was I born? Where had I gone to school? Where did I work? Every single answer I gave her was false except for the address on the license. I told her, for instance, that I worked at Liberty Bell

Racetrack in Philadelphia, selling programs, and had done that for three years. I told her that I had gone to Cherry Hill High School. For my home phone, I gave her a pay phone in a remote area.

Two hours later, I sat in an empty room that had a TV monitor. I was in a chair, the judge was on the screen. I watched as the pre-bail investigator gave the judge her recommendation. She told the judge she'd checked my background and recommended that I be released on personal recognizance so I could immediately return to work.

"This man is a responsible member of the community, Your Honor," she said. "I do not regard him as any threat to circumvent the jurisdiction of this court."

"Bail granted," he said, in a monotone.

Clearly, she had checked nothing. Amazing.

I packed up and left Philadelphia immediately, before anybody had a chance to connect Edward Davis to Craig Barry Jacob and his fugitive status. I now drifted from one city to another. Alexandria, Virginia; Hollywood, Florida; Chicago. In Chicago, I hit Procter & Gamble big.

It started with three of those product rebate checks. Two-dollar checks drawn on a bank in Ohio. I'm a bug for coupons and rebates. As I was looking over the rebate check, an idea occurred to me. I mean, to you one of these checks might have looked like it was a mere two bucks; to me it looked like a jackpot.

I called the bank on which the check was drawn and told the operations officer there that I was from John Deere Company and that I had a check in the amount of twenty-five thousand dollars that I wanted to be sure was good. I rattled off the account number on the rebate checks and, after the bank officer punched it into his computer, he told me: "That check is very good, sir."

I flew to New York the very next day and caught the subway to Brighton Beach in Brooklyn. There was a loan shark there who agreed to lend me nine hundred dollars. Back on the subway, I rode into Manhattan. I had the Procter & Gamble check in my pocket when I walked into a print shop on 34th Street, near Sixth Avenue.

I knew the owner and told him I needed to speak to him in private.

"What's up, man?" he asked, in his back office.

I told him I needed the Procter & Gamble checks altered so as to read twenty thousand dollars rather than two dollars.

"No problem," he said.

Six hours and five hundred dollars later, I had my checks. I flew to Cincinnati, where I opened up an account at The First Ohio Bank, Procter & Gamble's bank, using bogus ID that I'd bought for ten dollars on 42nd Street...and a one-hundred-dollar cash deposit.

The following day I deposited one of the twenty-thousand-dollar checks at First Ohio. The next day I called the bank as soon as it opened and checked my balance: twenty thousand one hundred dollars, they told me I had. All of the money, I was told, was available. The reason was the Procter & Gamble check was drawn on the same bank that I had my account with. That day, I drove to one of the bank branches and withdrew ten thousand dollars in traveler's checks. That evening, I withdrew most of the rest from a local mall branch office. The next day I caught a flight to Vegas, and in three and a half hours turned the traveler's checks into cash.

I lost some of the dough in Vegas, and within weeks the rest of it gambling in Chicago. So I phoned First Ohio to ask about my balance. To my surprise, the bank still did not realize that I had beaten them for almost twenty grand. I knew this from the polite way they spoke to me when they told me

I had a balance of three hundred eighty dollars. That was the exact amount I had left in the account. I also checked the Procter & Gamble account and found that I could hit it again.

I caught a bus to Cincy from Chicago. I get a bit paranoid about airports because FBI guys tend to loiter there. En route to Cincy, the bus stopped in Indianapolis, where most of the passengers exited. Four of the passengers sat in the front of the bus; I was alone in the rear. About twenty minutes out of Indianapolis, the bus stopped in a small town, where a black woman—cute, with a big radio—got on. With thirty or more empty seats on the bus, she asked if she could please sit next to me. I gave her a look like she was crazy, but moved toward the window and said "sure." It didn't take long before she lit up a joint and the two of us smoked it together, with me opening the window so as not to draw attention. Then without so much as a hint, Gloria reached inside my trousers and squeezed my penis.

"Where are you headed?" she asked.

"Cincinnati."

"I'm supposed to get off the stop before, but I'd love to spend the night with you."

We spent two nights at a Holiday Inn in Cincy. I hadn't been looking for sex; my gambling was consuming me. But once Gloria became available, I became interested.

It was a great couple of days. Gloria and the First Bank of Ohio. I screwed them both. Twenty-five grand off the Procter and Gamble account, all in cash, using five branch withdrawals.

Gloria reminded me of Helen. It was eighteen months since I threw Helen out of my apartment and sent her home to her mom's in Jacksonville for siccing the FBI on me. Nobody ever accused me of being bright about women: I called Helen and told her I wanted her back.

# It's one thing to have

phony checks; it's another to find a bank to cash them when you are a virtual stranger.

Let me tell you about split deposits.

A split deposit is where you take a bogus check and deposit only part of it in a newly-opened account. Part of the check goes into the account as a deposit, the rest the bank gives you as cash. Gives you as cash if you're smart enough to know the banks you're dealing with.

While I was in Chicago, I'd go to a library and look up banks in phone books. A prerequisite for me was a bank that had branches so that I could avoid becoming overly familiar to bank personnel. The rest had to do with demographics. In libraries you can find reference materials that would give the racial breakdown of a city. I'd avoid cities where there was a dense black and Hispanic population. Banks in those cities tended to be hip to the way split deposits could backfire. So I was looking for cities with predominantly white populations. I found them in Kalamazoo, Michigan, and in Madison, Wisconsin, and hit banks there for twenty-thousand-dollars worth of bogus-check split deposits. And decided it was time to move on. It was 1980. I was twenty-seven years old.

Helen and I got a sleeping car on an Amtrak to San Francisco. We never made it there, though. In Reno, I got lucky. My twenty grand turned into forty grand shooting craps. I decided Reno was for me.

"We're staying here," I told Helen.

"What about San Francisco?" she asked.

"Some other time. Reno feels right."

"Right for what?"

"For cashing in lots of chips."

And that was that.

Helen took a job at Harrah's as a cocktail waitress. I rented a nice garden apartment close to the downtown, and planned to keep my lucky streak going. Well, it didn't take long for reality to set in and my forty grand to dwindle to nothing. But that was when I hit on my next scam.

I'd hang around the sports books, occasionally betting the horses. While doing that I discovered that the casinos there would accept wagers even after races had begun. Past-posting, it's called. On busy days—weekends and holidays particularly—the tellers would still be accepting wagers as much as two, three, four minutes after post time.

I became friends with Ed and Gloria, a couple of window clerks in the race book at the Cal Neva casino in downtown Reno. Neither of them was what you'd call overpaid, so when I laid out my scheme for them they quickly agreed to be part of it.

I sent a guy named Lou—a degenerate gambler who lived in a motor home park in Reno—out to Los Angeles to rent a room at the Westerner Hotel, located across the street from Santa Anita race track. If you get the right room at the Westerner, you can see the races there so long as you have a good pair of binoculars. So the setup was I was in a pay phone booth at the Cal Neva and Lou was in his hotel room with his binocs and a bird's-eye view of the track.

As soon as I got the result of a race from Lou, I'd hurry to the race book and bet the winner. But at Cal Neva if the bet was over ninety-nine dollars, the clerk was obliged to report it to the head man there, Scotty Shackner. That didn't mean Scotty would crack down on you if you just happened to be lucky. But it did give him the opportunity to scope out any possible shenanigans that might be costing the casino serious money.

The way around this was to "box" your wager—bet the exacta, which allows you to "box" three horses with the objective of landing the first two finishers in the race. So let's say 1 and 2 finish first and second. What you do then is to box 1 and 2 with other numbers. Like 1 and 2 with 3, 1 and 2 with 4 and 1 and 2 with 6.

Now a half-smart clerk would see that this was a way to circumvent the ninety-nine-dollar quota and would bring it to Scotty's attention. But Gloria and Ed played it dumb when I cashed in my tickets.

Using Lou, I won five grand on two occasions, without complications. The next time I waited all day for a good exacta. It came in the ninth race and was worth twenty thousand dollars. But this time when I went to collect, Scotty was there.

"I notice, Jake, you're betting everything past-post," he said.

"I bet past-post a lot," I said, "and sometimes I win. How 'bout paying up on this one?"

"Yeah, we'll cash 'em this time. But I'm not gonna cash you past-post again."

"Why not?"

"You know why not."

"I don't know."

"You're smart, Jake. But you're not the only smart guy. It's the last time we cash you past-post. End of story."

And that night, Ed and Gloria were fired.

I took the sting out of their getting canned. We began past-posting as a team at other casinos. All three of us would place the same bet. Not for big money. Five, ten grand at a time and only when the casinos were crowded. We hit Harrah's and the Winner's Circle in Reno. MGM in Sparks. Caesars and Harrah's in Lake Tahoe. Artichoke Joe's in Carson City. When we sensed one place was getting on to us, we simply moved on to the next. In a couple of months, we had made about two hundred grand—one hundred twenty grand for me, forty grand apiece for Ed and Gloria. Lou got five hundred dollars a day. He wasn't all that bright a guy or ambitious about money.

It was a whirlwind few months, and exciting. I did not have much time for Helen, and in my fury to run the past-post scam to its limits, I didn't pay much attention to her. But toward the end of that period, she began hitting me up for sums of money that were out of whack with what I'd been giving her before. Because of that and her suddenly-erratic behavior, I knew she was on drugs. I didn't want to be bothered with the complications that a drug habit brings. One afternoon, she walked into the apartment, took off her clothes and began licking her lips.

She told me, "Baby, I need two hundred dollars."

She started kissing me passionately and undressing me with her hands. All of a sudden she stopped what she was doing and said, "You do have two hundred dollars, baby? Don't you?"

I told her I did, and after thirty minutes of excellent sex I gave her the money and she bolted from the apartment. I didn't need a ouija board to know where she was headed, or to know that she was potentially big trouble for me. I left her five hundred dollars and a note saying I was leaving for Chicago, adios.

What Helen did—as I pieced it together much later—was blow the five hundred dollars on drugs and, now broke, rat me to the cops. She told them I was a fugitive and I'd left her high and dry—she had no money to get home. But by the time she was in the precinct house telling her little tale, I was back out on the road. Not in Chicago, as I told her—that was just my little tale. Not in Chicago but in Los Angeles with my past-posting friend Ed.

With trips to the horse tracks and to Vegas, it didn't take us long to blow our money. This time I was really tapped out— no money for anything. And with no grand scam in mind, we had to come up with survival money.

Ed knew a woman at a Ramada Inn in Arcadia who'd run your credit card through and give cash so long as it was under fifty dollars. Under fifty dollars, she didn't need to get approval. I had a card in the name of Ellis Friedman, and she banged it three times at fifty dollars for a total of one hundred fifty dollars. While there, I checked out a list she had of credit card numbers that were no longer any good. My Ellis Friedman card was not yet on the list.

So with the card I began buying merchandise from various K marts and returning it for cash refunds. K mart didn't need a receipt to return goods. Under fifty dollars and if it had the

K mart sticker on it, it was good enough for them. There were ten K marts in the area. I was busy shuttling from one to the other, buying and returning merchandise for cash.

Pretty soon, we had a stake of nine hundred dollars and were heading back to Reno to do some more past-posting. By now, Lou had dropped out of sight so I had to figure out another way to get the results of the races. I phoned the press box at Aqueduct and asked for a horse-race writer from the *Newark Star-Ledger*, Bob Harding. I told Harding I was the son of Laz Barerra, a famous horse trainer.

Now I knew the fifth race at Aqueduct was being run as we spoke, but I pretended otherwise. I told Harding my horse, Ding Dong, was in the fifth race and I was curious how he had made out.

"Well, Barerra," Harding said, "the fifth is in progress as we speak. Hang on. I'll let you know how he does."

A minute passed, Harding came back on the wire: "Well, son. Your horse got fifth."

"Eh, too bad," I said. "Just curious, Bob. Who got first and second?"

With that information, I was back in the past-posting business. Or so I thought. But it turned out my previous success had led the casinos to be wary. By now the casinos had spotters looking over late arrivals at the betting windows, smart alecks like me with past-posting schemes. I found this out at Harrah's in Lake Tahoe when I tried to place a bet and was told the window was closed, even as a woman was placing a past-post bet at another window. I realized what had happened. They had my description, no question.

I changed my modus operandi.

I figured if I had innocuous-looking types bellying up to the window when I got the results, I could beat the casinos still. I called Gloria, and told her to put together a group of women who would place bets for me. She did that, and the next problem was how to communicate my inside information to them. I made up a code that converted letters to numbers and was preceded by the word "Doctor."

Here's how it worked. I'd call the press box at Aqueduct or some other track and, with a cock-and-bull story, wangle the first and second place finishers from a racing writer. Say the order of finish was horse #2 followed by horse #3. I then had "Dr. Barry Cook" paged in the race book. The B in Barry means horse #2 finished first, the C in Cook means horse #3 finished second. B, the second letter of the alphabet. C, the third letter of the alphabet. My lady in line makes the conversion and then bets those numbers, boxing 2 and 3 with other numbers. We tested it in Lake Tahoe and saw that it worked, then went to Vegas to make our killing.

We stung 'em. The Thunderbird, the Fremont, the Stardust, the Santa Anita Race Book, the Hollywood Race Book, the Sundowner Hotel. Better than two hundred thousand dollars we hit them for. Sometimes I'd get the winners from racetrack security people. They sit in a room with monitors that show the progress of a race. So they knew who the winners are. One of the Las Vegas papers carried a story about the Thunderbird getting nailed on a twenty-six-thousand-dollar past-posting scheme. That was me. I read it with a grin on my face. Soon after, none of the hotels would accept past-post wagers. Once again, I'd nailed a big institution to the wall and made it change how it did business.

There was one place in Vegas where I had problems. Place called Leroy's Race Book, next to the Fremont Hotel and Casino. Leroy's was owned by black guys. And when I hit them for ten grand and went to cash the ticket, the window clerk looked at me and called a big black guy, who came out from behind the cashier's cage with a baseball bat and told me, "I'm not cashing it."

He was a bad-looking hombre and I had the feeling that if I challenged him he might use that Louisville Slugger. So I ran out of the place. That night Ed and I were at the Plaza, a place downtown where they had night racing and where a lot of high rollers hung out.

My idea was to get one of them to cash the ticket. At the Plaza, I found one sport who was interested. We walked over to Leroy's and, by looking in the window of the now-closed betting parlor, he could verify the stamp was valid. Having done that, he paid me eight thousand dollars for the ticket. Whether he got his money, I never knew. Because Ed and I left Vegas that night for Sparks, a little town next to Reno.

In the Winners Circle there, we experienced a bit of misfortune. After I got the first and second finishers past-post, and bet them, it was announced the winner had been disqualified. That bit of news was costly. We'd invested twelve thousand five hundred dollars. So we were looking to come back strong. And did. Late in the day, we parlayed wagers totalling six grand into a jackpot of nearly one hundred thousand dollars. But the race book wouldn't pay, and wouldn't give a reason why. There was too much money involved for me to be intimidated. I demanded they ante up. They mumbled something about past-posting. I showed them the twelve-thousand-dollar losing ticket and said I'd lost money past-posting. They told me get stuffed—I wasn't gonna see any money.

"No chance, pal," the guy from the casino told me. "What I can authorize is eighteen thousand dollars to cover all the money you pumped into the window today."

"The hell with that," I said. "I want all the money."

"Try and get it," he said.

"I'll do better than try, pal. I'm gonna get the money. Watch and see."

"Whatever you say, sport."

I went before the state gaming commission and presented my case. They agreed that I had that money coming to me. They said they would contact the race book and get me my money. But the place closed soon after, and I never did see the dough.

It was 1981, and I was twenty-eight years old and about to find out how dumb I was about the oppposite sex.

# It happened in Reno,

where I won two thousand eight hundred dollars past-posting at Harrah's. Afterward, Ed and I had drinks at the casino bar. That's when security people converged on us and told me "Don't move." They'd noticed me from their security cameras, and realized that that was me in those pictures on their walls, thanks to my blabbermouth bimbo, Helen. Nine months earlier she had ratted me to the cops, and now the circle closed.

I was held in the Reno city jail for ten days until I was extradited to New York. The lawmen there wanted me for that old rap I'd run out on, the one instigated by Helen's call to the FBI. Well, this time I stood trial and ended up getting five years on the interstate stolen merchandise and another five years for bank fraud (lying on my loan applications), both terms to run concurrently.

I spent time in several joints, a good chunk of it in Petersburg, Virginia. In Petersburg, I got religion. I told prison officials that I was an Orthodox Jew and that I ate a kosher diet. There had been several recent law suits by Jewish inmates who wanted to maintain a kosher diet. The authorities at Petersburg wanted no part of litigation. So they acquiesced, giving me and the only other Jewish inmate there our own kitchen, plus a budget that enabled us to eat lamb chops, brisket, steak and potatoes while the rest of the prison population dined on rice and beans. My prison job became that of "kosher cook."

Once a week, a rabbi named Berkowitz came from Richmond to visit us. He was a contract rabbi, who went from joint to joint to spend time with incarcerated Jews. Usually, he'd tell us a little history and then talk about our families.

The kitchen became a kind of office for me. I had the keys and nobody else was supposed to enter there except for me and Stein, the other inmate of the Jewish persuasion. That provided me with excellent cover for the marijuana that I bought and sold...and for the football, basketball, and base-ball-pool tickets I distributed to inmates as part of my gambling operation there.

I was making at least one hundred dollars a week on the betting pool. This continued for six months and then a potential problem arose. One day a guy with a knife and another joker were about to jump me and steal my money when one of my aides, a guy named Quincy, intervened. Quincy was a karate expert. He kicked the knife out of the one guy's hand, and then punched out both of them. From that time on, everybody steered clear of me.

From Petersburg, I was shipped to Danbury. I had thirty months to go on my five-year sentence but was hoping to get parole. When I didn't, I got friendly with an inmate named

Marvin Marin, who was doing eleven years for embezzling eleven million. Marin was a jailhouse lawyer, very sharp, very smart. He helped me put together a persuasive argument for an early release, which I brought forth in federal court. I argued I was denied parole on hearsay, and the judge concurred. I was released from Danbury after six months—two years earlier than I was supposed to get out.

It was 1983. I was thirty years old and thrilled to get out early. My victory in the courts led me to form a company called Federal Consultants, whose objective was to serve inmates everywhere by filing papers on their behalf.

When I was paroled, I was ordered to live in a halfway house in midtown New York—43rd Street and Ninth Avenue. But the deal here was you shmeared the guy that ran the place—gave him a hundred bucks a week and that was that. You were free to live wherever the hell you wanted. For the guy—his name was Harvey—it was a sweet deal...while it lasted. Unfortunately for him, the authorities found out what he was doing and Harvey ended up going to prison.

Meanwhile, I was busy staffing Federal Consultants, hiring defrocked lawyers and jailhouse lawyers I'd met while doing time. As a group they were the original gang that couldn't shoot straight, but for a while we made money. We sent out fliers to prisons all across the country, offering a variety of services. For eight hundred dollars, we would file the papers requesting an inmate be allowed to transfer prisons, usually so he could be closer to home. Our success rate was pretty high on that procedure. For twelve hundred dollars, we would file papers for an earlier release or pursue a reduction in sentence. This was far more difficult to accomplish. Maybe in ten percent of the cases we succeeded.

Through another inmate-friend named Gregory, I began to get hold of bogus credit cards. Gregory had some Mafia pals who printed up these cards. Most guys who bought them used the cards on shopping sprees. In fact, there was a Radio Shack in Kings Plaza in Brooklyn that the goombahs hit so regularly that pretty soon the Secret Service set up shop there and began arresting one shmuck after another.

Not me. I went to Vegas and banged the cards for cash advances. In three days, with twenty-five different cards, under twenty-five different names, I made one hundred fifty thousand dollars. All you needed back then were a credit card and a driver's license. I had twenty-five cards and twenty-five licenses that matched the cards, drivers's licenses that had been stolen from the Department of Motor Vehicles.

Some cards had a twenty-thousand-dollar limit, others a two-thousand-dollar limit. Say you wanted five grand and the computer approved it. Then the computer would give the cashier an approval number. If the five grand was not available, then the machine would try to get an authorization code for descending numbers, in some cases for pissing money, practically. "You have two hundred dollars available, sir. Do you want it?"

The game was—take what you can, no matter how piddling an amount.

If a card ran out, no big deal. You were, as they say, "declined." That was it. No repercussions. Nothing. When that happened, I'd use stolen starter checks to repay the cards. These starter checks had no name on them. I'd put the name from the card on the check and that would allow me to start banging the card all over again. See, the bank would clear the check because you had a credit card with them. They wouldn't bother to check it out.

Funny thing was that none of the cards had a functioning magnetic strip. The Mafia guys' operation wasn't that sophisticated. But it didn't matter with the casinos. The cashiers would tell you, "Oh, your strip is damaged." So instead they'd punch your numbers into their computer by hand. Bing bang and—"Here's your money, sir." Piece of cake.

I asked one of my jailhouse lawyers if he knew a woman who could be an accomplice in a scam I had in mind. It was the old split-deposit routine, with a twist. I was targeting banks in the Lancaster, Pennsylvania, area, where they have a large Amish population and where, I figured, the banks— used to dealing with straight-up people—would be easier to dupe. Certainly in metropolitan New York, split deposits were a dead end. Unless a customer had available credit to cover the cash he wanted, there wasn't a chance in hell he was going to get it. But in Amish country I figured I could walk away with serious money.

The woman accomplice turned out to be Lorna. She was tall and busty, and sexy as hell—a child of a racially mixed marriage. She came from a family of jostlers—pickpockets. Lorna jostled once in a rare while. She was brighter than the others, and most of the time worked as a bookkeeper or computer operator. The moment I set eyes on her, I wanted her. But she gave no indication of being interested in me. Interested in my scam and in making money, yes. In me, not a glimmer.

I targeted a bank in Reading, Pennsylvania; we drove out there. She was puzzled when I told her we needed to go through the dumpster in back of the bank. I grabbed two bags of bank garbage and threw them into the trunk. Back in our motel room, I sorted out the garbage and came up with an account number that I could use—let's say the name on it was Susan Miller. I then made out a stolen blank check payable to our friend Miller in the amount of two thousand dollars. Lorna walked it in, making a split deposit. A thousand dollars into "her" account, the rest in cash. We worked the scam at ten branch banks and came home with ten thousand dollars.

Reading, Pennsylvania was a one-time thing, and then I was back into the credit cards.

Federal Consultants was not a money-maker. I felt sorry for inmates who could not afford the cost of the firm's services, so I accepted IOU's, which turned out to be worthless.

Then, out of the blue, Lorna phoned me one day.

"Jake, I need your help," she said.

"For what?"

She told me she had lost her job and needed money to pay the rent.

"Will you help me?" she asked.

"You mean, money?"

"No. I wouldn't ask you for money."

"What then?"

"We need someone to drive us."

"'Us?'"

"My brother, sister and me."

She needed me to drive them to a series of malls in and around Short Hills, New Jersey, where they planned to go on a jostling excursion. My cut would be twenty-five percent of the plunder. It sounded nickel-and-dime to me, but it got me close to Lorna again, so I agreed. In Reading, we had stayed over in a motel, but even though we had slept in the same bed, it was nothing-doing. She wouldn't let me lay a glove on her. But I had a torch for her still.

That day the group of them hit about a dozen stores, and lifted about twenty wallets. While I headed back to the Bronx, to drop three of them off, Lorna's brother and sister began collecting the money in the wallets. In my rear-view mirror, I could see Lorna's brother Eddie—dumb bastard— hiding money from me in his shoe.

"Whatcha doin', Eddie?" I said, while I drove.

"Nothin'," he said, looking chagrined.

"Nothin'?"

"That's right."

I just smiled to let him know I was hip to what he was doing.

My share of the day's thievery came to $498.88 and I told him I was aware he had shortchanged me. Not that it mattered, really. For me it was all about Lorna. Back in the Bronx, she invited me in. And then her brother, sister and a sexy number named Nicole—a friend of theirs—threw in to buy some crack cocaine. After a while, Eddie said he was hot and took off his shirt. Then Nicole took off her blouse, followed by Lorna. I felt a bit out of place. Not only was I fulled clothed, but I was the only one in the bunch who declined to smoke the crack. Instead I puffed on my cigar and drank Pepsi.

When the crack ran out, Nicole's money did too. So when Eddie, Lorna and her sister kicked in for more crack, Nicole asked me for a loan.

"You buy crack and then we can go to a motel, okay Jake?" she said.

I drove her to 145th Street, where she scored. On the way to the hotel in New Jersey, Nicole got stoned on the crack. Once we reached the hotel, she kept offering me a hit. The first few times I said no, but eventually I went for it, trying crack for the first time of my life. Nicole's lips met mine as she shot smoke from the crack pipe into my mouth. I liked it, and shared her crack until it ran out.

The following few months were full of cocaine and sex, in rooms where sometimes both occurred simultaneously. The people I was running with now were a wild bunch and I occasionally felt out of my element. But while it lasted, it was an eye-opener.

There were Cindy and Tricia, lesbians who liked getting it on while the rest of us watched. There was Mileak, a black nutcase who while on crack confessed: "I think I might have killed her, you know, when I grabbed her purse and stuck the knife in the bitch."

I watched, I listened, I did some crazy things myself. Like when my pal Gregory, who was doing time in Danbury, wanted marijuana, I slit open six tennis balls and put pot inside, then sealed the balls tightly. On a prearranged day, I had a guy drive up to the Danbury prison and, at precisely noon, throw the balls over the main building of the facility. Gregory had men spread out across the compound and, when the six balls landed on institution grounds, they were immediately retrieved and given to Gregory.

Soon after, Gregory was released, and he came to see me with a stolen check from a rich stockbroker's Marine Midland money market account. He wanted to know if I could do anything with the check. I made a phone call to Marine Midland and verified that the check was good for at least one hundred thousand dollars. Then I had Gregory wait outside my office while I called in an employee of mine, Leroy Carter.

Leroy was an ex-con who had done five years in Lewisburg for bank robbery. Since Leroy was on my company's payroll savings plan, I knew he had an account at Carteret Savings in New Jersey. Leroy now told me he'd had the account there for fourteen years, and that it presently held the grand sum of four hundred dollars.

"Leroy," I said, "you have a chance to make twenty thousand dollars illegally. It'll involve your bank account and there's a ten percent chance you wind up in jail for five years. You interested?"

"Yeah," he said. "I am."

The following day the check was made out to Leroy in the amount of one hundred thousand dollars, and later that day it went into Leroy's account via an express deposit box. The following morning I called the Carteret Bank to check Leroy's balance. The woman there told me the balance was $100,490.88 and the one hundred thousand of the amount would not be available for thirteen days.

Two weeks later, I put Leroy through extensive rehearsals. We went over all the possible questions he could be asked by bank tellers or officers. I was not about to have him withdraw the money in cash. No one in his right mind does. My plan was to send Leroy to ten different branch banks and at each to submit a withdrawal slip for ten thousand dollars and request traveler's checks. By the following day, Leroy and I had our hundred thousand dollars.

That afternoon, we drove to Atlantic City and then Leroy went from casino to casino cashing the traveler's checks. Each time he got his money, he'd hand it over to me. On our drive back to New York, I gave Leroy his twenty grand. He didn't question why he was only getting the twenty, though if he had I was prepared to tell him that five people were involved and each of us was getting an equal split.

The following day Leroy showed up at work as if nothing happened. That day I drilled him for hours. I told him that he would definitely be arrested and I explained to him what he was to tell the FBI when the time came.

A few weeks later, he was taken in for questioning by the FBI. He proceeded to tell the feds the story I had given him. He told the FBI that he had won the one hundred thousand dollars in a high-stakes card game in Brooklyn. The man who lost the one hundred grand had no more cash when Leroy won the pot; it was either take a check or nothing.

Leroy said he had no idea at that moment whether the check was good, so he had phoned the bank and told them of his dilemma. On the recommendation of the bank, he said, he deposited the check in his account and waited to see if it would clear. When it did, he decided to parlay it into a rich-for-life gambling spree in Atlantic City by withdrawing the money. But, he told the G-men, the bank would not let him withdraw all the money at once without three day's notice. So he had done it ten thousand dollars at a time, in traveler's checks, at ten of the branches, and then had blown the entire sum gambling in Atlantic City.

That was the story he told the FBI, and the story he continued to tell when he went to trial in Newark, New Jersey. And guess what? The government couldn't put a dent in that tale. Leroy was acquitted of charges.

In the weeks that followed, I got more involved with Lorna and her pickpocketing brothers and sisters.

They were slick at lifting wallets. They worked like a team, usually in supermarkets in New York City. Lorna would walk behind an unsuspecting shopper as the woman wheeled her cart. Typically, the woman would have her pocketbook in the kiddy seat of the shopping cart. Then one of Lorna's brothers would materialize on the woman's other side. He'd be wearing thick, geekish eyeglasses and, as he reached for a can on the shelf, he'd turn to the woman and say: "I don't see so good. Can you read the ingredients for me? I'm a Muslim and not allowed to eat pork." While the shopper was reading from the can, Lorna would unsnap the woman's pocketbook, snatch her wallet and, smooth as can be, snap the pocketbook up again. That way, the woman wouldn't know her wallet had been lifted until she was at the check-out counter, ready to pay.

Anyway, where I came in was at the end of their working day. Before me, they would take the dozen or so wallets they'd lifted, strip them of cash and then dump the wallets. They didn't really know how to get mileage out of the credit cards. They asked me to help them.

Because of Lorna, I did.

I knew the 800 number for Comchek, the company that authorized credit card transactions. Comchek was in Memphis. And once Lorna and her brothers and sisters took the cash from the wallets, I'd call, pretending to be in Atlantic City. Each casino had a location number with Comchek—a number that was visible by the cash machines. I'd give the location number and ask for my cash advance, practically minutes after the wallet was lifted...and before the victims had a chance to report the cards stolen.

Then we would drive to Atlantic City, arriving two to three hours after I'd phoned Comchek. The money would be waiting for us at whatever location I'd designated—in the form of a check that you would sign and for which the casino would give you cash. Sometimes the cashier would wonder why it had taken us so long to get the money.

"I got lucky on a roll of quarters," I'd say. "I hit the slots for one hundred dollars."

It was an excuse that made sense to them, and they'd give a patronizing smile.

That Atlantic City cash pickup would have satisfied most folks. Not me, though. I didn't want those cards to die on the way to Atlantic City. To extend their life, I came up with this twist: I'd call the cardholder.

"Hello, this is Sgt. Bill Lee from the Port Authority police," I'd say. "We just arrested somebody who had your credit cards."

"Great," the victim would say. "I was just robbed at Key Food."

"Well, we've nailed the guy, and everything in your wallet appears intact. But I'd like to go over the contents with you to be absolutely sure."

I'd then give them a rundown on all their cards. The idea was to make them assume their cards were safe and they need not report them as stolen. If they bought the bullshit, it could mean several days more to whack up those cards.

Sometimes, the victim would suggest she come down to Port Authority Police and pick up the card.

"I wish you could, ma'am," I'd say. "But as soon as I hang up, I'm going off duty. I'm going to put your wallet in the mail and you'll have it in a day or two."

Eventually, I began living with Lorna. She had gotten arrested and had phoned me to help her get out of jail. She needed three thousand dollars to make bail. I didn't have the money, but told her no sweat—I'd be there the next morning. And then I tried to figure out how I was going to come up with three grand. Like magic, the money showed up in my mail that afternoon—a gold MasterCard with a ten-thousand-dollar limit.

I bailed her out the next day and then drove her to a building in Elizabeth, N.J.

"What's this?" she asked.

"Where we're going to live," I told her.

I'd rented a furnished apartment for us. Lorna was skeptical as we got out of the car, but once inside she underwent a quick attitude adjustment.

"Geez, this is great," she said.

We bought crack, made love, the following day she moved her belongings in.

A few weeks later, I was in my office when a goodlooking brunette walked in. She said her name was Rita Manley and she asked for a job. The business was going to hell—what with all the druggies I had working for me—so I had no job to offer her. But she was very charming, not to mention sexy. We talked; one thing led to another. That weekend a bunch of us from the office, Rita included, had a cocaine party at a house I had bought for forty thousand dollars down in Staten Island, a house Lorna knew nothing about.

A crazy weekend it was. Rita and I made love. Gregory showed up and asked me to hold an Uzi of his overnight—he was afraid the cops were staking out his place in Brooklyn. While I stepped out for a while, the Uzi disappeared. I threatened violence if it didn't reappear. It reappeared. Eventually, the party ended, everybody split. I went out for breakfast. When I came back—trouble.

On my street, where there were rarely any cars, I saw my house was under surveillance—there were unmarked cars everywhere. Rather than turn onto the street, I drove past, to a nearby mall, and pulled out a pair of binoculars I used at the horse tracks. From where I stood, I could see everything. The cars stayed there about an hour and then a locksmith's truck appeared. I watched as the locksmith disconnected the alarm system and the authorities went into my house. They didn't emerge until a good hour-and-a-half later. Eventually, the cars pulled out; I returned home.

On my refrigerator were four search warrants signed by a Brooklyn magistrate, enabling the DEA, FBI and the Tobacco and Firearms people to rummage through my place. Rita Manley, it turned out, was working for the FBI, DEA and New Jersey police. She'd cut a deal for herself after being arrested on a cocaine charge. One of my Federal Consultant jailhouse lawyers was set up by her for drug possession, a violation of his parole.

When news of my owning a house in Staten Island reached my parole officer, he threatened to violate me. I argued it with him, but I suspected the worst was about to happen and decided to take it on the lam again rather than being sent back to the joint.

This time Lorna went with me. It was March 1985 and we headed for Tampa, Florida.

# In Tampa, I assumed a

new identity, that of David Goldstein. I had a counterfeit credit card and a bogus driver's license under that name, Lorna a phoney driver's license as Lorna Goldstein.

David Goldstein was a real person who resided in Short Hills, New Jersey, with his wife and two children. He was an attorney for a large corporation.

Before bolting New Jersey, I had stopped at Trans Union in Queens and TRW in New Jersey and obtained credit reports on Goldstein. With these reports, I now knew everything I needed to know about him, so that I could live under that name. I knew his college, his previous employer, his social security number. I knew every credit card he and his wife held and the limit on each of the cards. I knew the name of the bank that held his mortgage and the balance owed on his home in Short Hills.

The first thing I did in Tampa after purchasing a home was to obtain a valid Florida driver's license. I then opened a checking and saving account with the "Landmark Bank" that held the mortgage on my home. Within weeks, the bank sent me a new Visa card. Once I was listed in the phone book, I filled out an American Express application and told them I had been in business for twenty years. Fourteen days later, I had a David Goldstein American Express card. A week later, Sun Bank sent me a Visa card without my even asking for it.

I was established now. I had an office on Dale Mabry Boulevard and was handing out cards as "David Goldstein, Esq." That's right. I'd opened a law firm, a natural offshoot, I figured, of the legal advisory business for convicts I'd had up north.

The business in Tampa never amounted to much. There were too many horse tracks and jai alai frontons to occupy my time...and money. Within three weeks, my bankroll was gone and I was in debt five thousand dollars to a local bookie.

Gregory came to the rescue, sending me five counterfeit credit cards with matching driver's licenses. Lorna and I flew to Nassau with the new cards and registered at a Club Med resort as Mr. and Mrs. Weinberg. In two days, we banged the five cards for eighteen thousand dollars, then drove out to the Paradise Island casino.

Lorna played the slots while I shot craps. At one point I was up thirty thousand dollars, but after three days I had gone flat bust, even going through the eight hundred dollars that was left on my so-called legit Landmark Visa. I went over to give Lorna the bad news. But I never got a chance to. For as I approached her slot machine, bells started ringing: Lorna had just hit the jackpot. The casino let the bells ring for twenty minutes, then paid her three thousand nine hundred dollars. She held on to one hundred dollars to keep playing, and gave me the rest.

There were six hours to go before our plane was to depart Nassau for Florida. So I took the money to the craps table and in three hours I had increased it to nineteen thousand dollars. Nineteen grand! Soon after, we headed for the airport, both of us exhilarated by our good fortune at the tables. But like-that, we suddenly found ourselves in a pickle when the Bahamian police detained us.

That morning, when my quick checkout at the hotel was processed, the hotel tried to get an approval for three hundred forty dollars on my Landmark Visa. The authorization was denied. Since I had had eight hundred dollars when I registered—money I'd subsequently used to gamble—the hotel thought I was trying to beat them and called the police.

At the precinct house, the cops acted as though we were deadbeats.

"Let's go, mahn, empty your pockets," one of the officers instructed me.

I did. Very slowly. Letting him get fucking goggle-eyed over the wad I pulled out.

"How am I doing?" I asked, straight-faced.

Nineteen thousand dollars—probably more than he earned in a year. Soon after, the manager of the hotel arrived and I paid him three hundred forty dollars in cash. I then drew a police escort to the Avis office, where I was told to pay my bill in cash.

What had been a potential hard time ended without a fuss.

But back in Tampa we decided it was time to move on. I flew out to Los Angeles and found a house in Lakewood—a house for rent, with an option to buy. Then I returned to Tampa. Lorna and I sold the place in Tampa for a small loss, packed our things and drove west. In the Best Western Hotel in Orange, Texas, we made love in the swimming pool, and nine months later our first child, Jeanne, was born.

In Lakewood, the Goldsteins became the Gelmans. Had to because we had maxed all the credit cards we had as Goldstein. I'd even sent Lorna to the bank to use our checking-plus feature for a farewell five thousand bucks.

Anyway. I found my new identity, Norman Gelman, through the TRW machine at Allstate Trading, where I worked briefly. Norman, bless him, had twenty years of excellent credit that I could exploit. Had I lived a moderate life, Lorna (who was earning eighteen thousand dollars a year at Kelly Girl, to supplement the fifty-two thousand dollars I was earning with Allstate Trading) and I would have been very comfortable.

But given my gambling habit, it didn't take long for me to get myself in deep shit. I owed a bookie in Los Angeles twenty-three grand and another in New York five grand, and both of them wisely cut me off while pressuring me to pay up. To get out of that jam, I put the sting on People's Express Airlines.

Remember People's Express? It was an airline that flew out of Newark. Its Newark-Los Angeles flight was considered a real bargain—ninety-nine dollars off-peak and either one hundred forty-nine dollars or one hundred ninety-nine dollars at peak hours—about half of what other commercial airlines charged.

I had shuttled back and forth on People's flights on clandestine visits to my parents. Because I was a fugitive, they contacted me on an 800 beeper and we made our arrangements to see one another that way. While doing that, I noticed that People's was susceptible. The reason? Passengers paid their fares on the plane, and the airlines didn't bother to check the validity of the credit cards used. The stewardesses just ran the card through the imprinting machine and you were paid.

Because People's Express's fares were so cheap, there was always a scarcity of seats. Reservations had to be made way in advance. I had five bogus credit cards and driver's licenses. What I did with the credit cards was to make ten reservations for each flight I took—Newark to Los Angeles and Los Angeles to Newark. Then, when I got to the airport, I'd locate the standby passengers. With the cheap fares, there was always a mob of them, particularly on a Friday.

By then I'd have checked in and would have ten passes with "Gelman" on all of them. I'd go over to the standby line and tell them: "I have extra seats on the plane."

Well, the news would set off a kind of feeding frenzy. Those folks would surround me, pushing and jostling for my attention. I'd have the tickets sold in a blink. Once aboard, I'd pay for all the tickets with bad credit cards and pocket the money that my standbys gave me.

I worked the scam for six weeks and hit People's Express for more than forty thousand dollars. It wasn't easy work. Constant coast-to-coast flights. One day, as I retrieved my luggage, I saw a few supervisors huddling by the baggage area, pointing to me. I figured all they knew was I was selling tickets for a profit. If they had been aware of my bogus method of payment I doubt they would have been as laid-back about it.

Even so, their finger-pointing made me uneasy. Very uneasy. When I got my bag, one of them shouted, "Excuse me, sir. Would you come here, please?"

Hell no. I was out of there in a flash and never flew the airline again. In this business it's fatal to overstay your welcome.

One funny postscript. When the standby passengers paid me, it was usually in cash. Once in a while I'd accept a check. Well, in one instance, a Chinese guy travelling with his two sons stuck me with a bum check. When it bounced, I called the bank. They told me the guy was on the run, leaving a trail of bad checks everywhere.

The bank suggested we work together to catch this guy. That tickled me. Scam man on the trail of the prick that scammed him.

"The last thing we have on him is he used his AmEx in El Monte, California, three days ago," the guy from the bank said.

"Is that right?" I said.

"Yup. So he's in your area. What do you say to helping us?"

Said no.

## Back in Lakewood,

I came up with a scheme to beat Western Union. I had heard that you could wire money on your Visa or MasterCard over the telephone. All you needed was a legit credit card number. That was easy. I'd put on a jacket and tie and go out to Los Angeles Airport, the PSA counter, and stand next to travellers as they checked in—stand next to them as if I had to ask the airline clerk a question. But what I was doing was catching the numbers of their credit cards, which I would immediately write down.

Sometimes in Vegas, I'd watch people use their cards in casino cash machines. With some of those machines in those days, the numbers would light up on the screen. All you had to do was sit at a discreet distance and jot them down.

I had other legit card numbers from a woman named Sissy, who worked for Hertz and was not averse to selling me valid MasterCard and Visa numbers, with all the information about the person that was on the contract. I had offered her ten dollars per rental agreement; she'd xeroxed two hundred of them. Practically a lifetime supply.

Some of those cards would help me scam Western Union. The way it worked, you phoned Western Union and told them how much money you needed to wire. Two thousand five hundred dollars per transaction was their max. But if a card had a twenty-thousand-dollar limit, you could call back and request two thousand five hundred dollars, seven more times. Western Union sent the money only if you called from your home or place of employment. That way they could phone you back and be satisfied you were who you said you were.

Okay. So I would call and tell them I wanted to send two thousand five hundred dollars.

Western Union would ask for my credit card number and to whom the money was going.

"And can I have the number you're calling from...is that home or business?"

If you said it was neither, Western Union would reply, "Sorry, can't send it. You have to go to your home or business phone."

What I would do is phone them from a place like the Broadway, a department store in Los Angeles. I'd find a phone not being used—say in men's wear—and place the following call:

"Hi. This is Joe Blow. I'd like to send two thousand five hundred dollars to Norman Gelman and I'm at work. You can call me at the Broadway, extension such and such."

And I'd give them the main number for the store.

Then, in a suit and tie, I'd stand by that phone and pick it up on the first ring: "Hello. Broadway Store. Mr. Blow speaking."

"Hello. This is Western Union calling. Just verifying you work for the Broadway. The money is being sent."

Western Union would ask where the money was going. But it didn't matter what you said. You could, for instance, give an address in New York City, then go around the corner in Los Angeles and get the money. Once your name was on the computer, you could pick up the money anywhere.

I hammered Western Union with this scheme for about six weeks, using different stores. The Broadway, the May Company, Neiman Marcus. All the biggest stores. It worked like a charm. Over those six weeks, I scored twenty thousand dollars.

One day I didn't receive a return call while standing at the counter of a department store. When I called back on a store pay phone, I was told: "Sir, you don't work for the store. I just called personnel. If you want to send money, call us back from your home."

Well, it had taken them a while to get hip to me. But that didn't discourage me. I beat the chumps anyway. Here's how.

In Los Angeles there are stores called Target—they're cheap goods stores similar to K mart. I picked one not far from my home in Lakewood, put on a suit and tie and entered while carrying a briefcase.

Lorna went with me, but not into the store. From a pay phone outside, she phoned the main number at Target and asked for John Miller.

"Hello," she said, "this is Mrs. Green from the Milwaukee office. I'm John Miller's secretary. Mr. Miller is district manager and is in your store at present. Would you please page him?"

When I heard the page, I walked over to the front counter.

"Yes, I'm Mr. Miller."

"We didn't know you were in the store, sir," she said. "There's a call for you on line three."

Lorna and I went through a previously-rehearsed conversation and I hung up.

"Thank you very much," I told the girl at the front counter.

I then stepped outside and, from a pay phone, contacted Western Union as John Miller and asked them to wire five grand to the name on a bogus credit card and driver's license in my possession. I told them Target was my employer.

Minutes later, I was paged again while in Target.

The woman at the counter said that Western Union had just called to confirm that I worked for Target and she had assured them I did.

It's weird the way these swindles occur to me. It's like a nerve end gets activated and suddenly my mind's in overdrive—and I'm just there for the ride. It happened like that soon after the Western Union jackpot, on a trip I made from Los Angeles to New York.

Lorna asked if I would send her brother Sam, who was serving a prison sentence in upstate New York, a money order on his commissary account. When I got to New York, I stopped in at a Citibank branch for a money order. But I erred when I made the money order out to me instead of Sam. I realized my mistake as soon as I made it and, when I got to the window, I explained it to the teller. She directed me to a bank officer, saying he would approve the money order for cash and she could start all over again.

I stepped over to the bank officer's desk and told him what had happened.

"No problem," he said, initialing the money order.

The bank officer then walked over to the teller's window and said to the head teller, who I assumed was his wife: "It's 1:00, dear. Let's go to lunch."

And off they went.

While I was standing in line, I had a brainstorm. I put the money order in my pocket and just bought another fifty-dollar money order, which I mailed to Lorna's brother.

The following day I rented a car and drove to Brooklyn, where I contacted a guy who had a supply of business checks.

"The account on these checks is closed," he said.

"Doesn't matter," I told him.

He shrugged and gave me the checks free of charge on account of past favors I had done him. But I did pay him fifty dollars for a bogus license that the guy made conform to my description.

I drove over to Macy's and used their floor-model typewriters to make the check out in the amount of ten thousand dollars. I then copied the initials from the back of the fifty-dollar money order I had kept, onto the back of the phony ten-thousand-dollar check.

Back to Citibank I drove. I parked and waited, hoping that the bank officer who had okayed the money order for cash would come strolling out the bank at 1 P.M. My luck, he did— in the company of his wife. It was Friday afternoon and the bank was crowded. It took me fifteen minutes to get to the window. Once there, I handed the teller the check.

"It's already been approved," I said, "and I'd like to get the entire amount in cash."

The teller glanced at the initials on the back of the check, stamped it and put it with the rest of her checks. It took the teller a few minutes to count out the ten grand in one-hundred dollar bills and have me recount it, and then I was gone.

Here's the kicker. Later that day, I flew to Las Vegas and blew the ten grand. Which meant I still had money problems by the time I got back to Lakewood.

No sweat. From the Visa and MasterCard rental agreement forms I'd bought from that agent at Hertz, I plotted the next variation of Western Union trickery. I now sorted through that batch and zeroed in on six names. The first was a Frank Esposito from West Covina. With his agreement in front of me, I picked up the phone and called the Pacific Bell business office.

"Hi. This is Frank Esposito," I said, giving them Esposito's home phone number. "I'd like to add call forwarding to my service. How long will it take?"

"Three days, sir. Will that do?"

"Great."

The following week, I drove to a mall in West Covina and phoned Esposito from a pay phone there.

"Mr. Esposito. This is Norman Gelman from Pacific Bell. I need your help in clearing some phone lines in the area."

"Be glad to help you, Mr. Gelman. What do you want me to do?"

I gave him a number to dial, then told him to wait for the dial tone and dial 244-0090. By following my instructions he was transferring his phone calls from his home phone to a phone located in the mall. When he did as I asked, I was on the other end of the phone as it rang in the mall.

"Pacific Bell and Repair," I answered. "Thanks for your help, Mr. Esposito. For the next hour or so, you may get some single rings on your line. Just ignore them while we clear up our little problem."

With Esposito compliant, I was now ready, once again, to abuse old faithful, Western Union. When I called, I gave Esposito's Visa number and then his home phone, which Western Union then verified with directory assistance. Western Union then phoned me back, approving the credit card transaction.

I repeated the same scheme five minutes later, using Esposito's home number and credit card, but this time I called Comchek, a Western Union competitor. No problem. They approved a money transfer, and the money, two thousand five hundred dollars, was quickly available at offices throughout America.

I kept going through my list of six Hertz rental agreements, enjoying the same success I'd had with Esposito. It wasn't until the sixth name on the list that I experienced problems.

Her name was Leah Tambor and she was from Belair, California. A sixty-year-old woman living alone. As before, I had asked the phone company to have call forwarding added to her service. But in several attempts to get Miss Tambor to forward her calls, I had been unsuccessful.

"Are you sure you're doing EXACTLY what I tell you?" I asked.

"Absolutely."

"Then why are we having these troubles?"

"Well, how would I know," she said. "You're the one that works for Pacific Bell."

I was certain she was screwing up my instructions. I got so disgusted that I got into my car, drove to Sears Roebuck and bought a jumpsuit and a box of tools. I then drove to Leah's house.

"Howdy, ma'am," I said. "I'm Ted Maxwell from Pacific Bell. I'm a repair supervisor and one of my men reported you're having problems forwarding calls so that he can clear some lines in the area."

"That's right," she said, "and he sure was testy about it."

"I apologize for his behavior. May I come in and see if I can solve this problem?"

She invited me in.

"Can you direct me to the nearest phone?" I said.

She took me into the living room and pointed to a rotary phone on a coffee table.

"Are there other phones?" I asked.

"Yes."

She showed me them—all rotary phones. Now I understood the problem. Call forwarding worked only with push-button phones.

"May I make a suggestion?" I said. "Your rotary phone set-up isn't adaptable to the procedures we need to use to clear up our line problems. What Pacific Bell would like to do is make you a gift of a push-button phone."

She was suspicious: "What do you mean a 'gift?' "

"Free of charge," I said.

"I'll want a receipt that says that," she said.

"No problem, ma'am. Be pleased to give you one."

I drove back to Sears and bought a push-button phone and then returned to Leah's house. I plugged in the phone and then activated call forwarding. Lorna was at a pay phone a mile from the house, waiting.

"That does it," I said. "Now Miss Tambor, there may be a few single rings. You just ignore them til we get our little problem solved. Shouldn't take more than an hour."

I started to leave.

"Young man," she said, "you're forgetting something."

"Ma'am?"

"My receipt."

I wrote her out a receipt.

"This better be good," she said, waving the receipt. "Because I have no intention of paying for that phone. I was perfectly content with my other phone."

"No charge whatsoever," I assured her. "You're a valued customer, Miss Tambor, and we're only too happy to improve your service."

"Well, I never knew the telephone company to give away something for free."

I gave a little wave and hurried out to my car. I met up with Lorna at the pay phone, where she called Comchek and Western Union.

Both transactions were approved and we picked up the cash the following day.

Now if you're thinking—what a heel, ripping off an old lady—relax. It didn't work that way. Leah did not lose anything, she gained a fifty-dollar push-button phone. The loser was Western Union and Comchek.

In the beginning, when I used Visa and MasterCard to get money off either Comchek or Western Union, the banks absorbed the loss. But they began to rethink their responsibility and decided that Western Union's security was lax and they advised Western Union that in the future they would no longer bear the brunt of that company's problems.

# All the years that Lorna

and I were on the run, we never lacked for material posses-sions. There were times when I might be as much as fifty thousand dollars in the hole, but somehow, some way, I always managed to come up with a scheme that would can-cel my debt and put money, big money in my pockets.

But while in Fremont, I began to wish I could live a more normal life. I knew that meant curbing my gambling addic-tion, and for a while I tried. Without much success.

Just the same, I made a big push toward going straight, deciding that I would start up a business and see if I could make a go of it. To do that, though, required some working capital. And as well-meaning as I was, the only way I could get that money quickly was to come up with a not exactly legitimate scheme.

My target was Household Finance. My objective: secure a loan, using a bogus identity. The man I pretended to be was real enough. I'd used TRW's credit report on him to bone up on his history. When I phoned Household Finance, and applied for a ten-thousand-dollar personal loan as this "Michael Kent," I had his TRW report in front of me. So it was no problem supplying all the personal details Household Finance wanted: name, address, employer, credit card numbers. The tricky part was their request for a number at which they could get back to me. I told them that I was a repairman for Pacific Bell—which Michael Kent was—and that the job took me out on the road. So the best thing would be for me to phone them. When I reached them later that day, the news was good. My loan had been approved.

"Just bring your driver's license for identification purposes," they told me.

"Okay," I said, and hung up.

I didn't have a driver's license as Michael Kent. What I did was to drive to the motor vehicle department in San Francisco and grab one of those learn-to-drive booklets. At the bottom of the booklet the department's main office in Sacramento was listed, with a phone number. With a scissors, I cut that out and pasted it to a white piece of paper that I xeroxed. I now was in possession of what looked like a piece of stationery from the Department of Motor Vehicles in Sacramento.

I then typed a letter, supposedly from Motor Vehicles to Michael Kent, advising him his license was under suspension for two more months and warning him of the consequences if he was caught driving during that time. In the letter, I layered in his date of birth and his driver's license number.

With that letter I walked into Household Finance offices in and around San Francisco. I'd go over the details of the loan—how much it would cost, so on so forth. They'd have me sign in a number of places. Half the time they didn't even bother to ask for my driver's license. They'd just hand me a check. The rest of the time, when they asked for the driver's license, I'd give them the letter from Sacramento.

"This is embarrassing," I'd say, "but it's all I have."

It never failed. I'd have Household Finance phone ahead to their bank so I could walk right in and cash the check.

"I'd like you to tell 'em I'm coming down there," I'd say. "I kind of want to keep this quiet because I'm using the money to surprise my wife—take her on an anniversary trip."

I ended up getting sixty thousand dollars out of this Household Finance scheme, money that enabled me to found Pacific Collection Service. The office was located in San Francisco, and Lorna, the baby and I lived a ways out from the city, in Fremont.

Pacific was a collection agency—we collected on bad checks—a bit of irony there. For every check we received money for, we would keep fifty percent.

The way it worked is that through TRW we would locate the individual's employer and phone him there.

"Look," we'd say, "we can put your name in the computer and list you as a bad credit risk, or we can try to work this out if you want."

Sometimes we'd agree to take as little as ten dollars a week.

Through an ad I placed, Mike Garcia, a very persuasive salesman, came aboard, lured by my offer of twenty-five percent of the business. He was well worth the percentage I gave him. Right away, he nailed a couple of supermarket accounts, Safeway and Lucky's. It didn't stop there. One day, Mike was in a supermarket in San Francisco, picking up bad checks, when a guy there said to him: "You people ought to clear coupons for supermarkets. There's big money in that." The supermarket guy offered our company a coupon-clearing account worth two hundred fifty thousand dollars a year.

"What do you think?" Mike asked me later that day.

I did my research and found there were nine major clearing houses across the country that handled manufacturer's coupons. I called one of them and said I represented Safeway and was looking for a new clearing house—could I get a tour of their factory? An appointment was set up for the following day.

The sales rep for the clearing house showed me the entire operation, explaining what his company did every step of the way. I decided we could make a buck in this business: On July 1, 1986, I renamed my company Pacific Clearing House and Collection Agency. Mike proceeded to round up the accounts. During our first month we received one-million-dollars worth of coupons to clear.

Both Mike and I worked sixteen hours a day, sorting coupons by manufacturer, mailing them out and keeping the books straight. After a while, we hired ten deaf mutes to work for us, paying them $4.35 an hour to sort coupons. We hired a bookkeeper and then an accountant. We signed a contract with an attorney. We hired two typists and two couriers and then a mailroom clerk. We had a receptionist as well as a private secretary. It wasn't long before we had about eighty employees and were operating twenty-four hours a day.

For a while business went well. So well, in fact, that I became a kind of pillar in the community, believe it or not. Folks in Fremont knew about my hiring deaf mutes and considered me a civic-minded swell fellow. I was treasurer of the Kiwanis, a regular at Junior Chamber of Commerce meetings and, with Lorna, a member of the local tennis club. The relationships with my employees were excellent: they were frequent guests at my home. If they had problems they could come to me. I lent them money. I'd co-sign for their autos, their homes, their loans. I was everybody's best friend.

I don't know if this was the happiest time of my life. But I sure felt comfortable. I had an excellent credit rating and, besides the home in Fremont, there was a getaway place in Lake Tahoe. I loved the lifestyle that I was living. Lorna and I went boating on the lake, as well as fishing and water ski-ing. Best of all, of course, was the availability of the casinos. If not for the fact that we were on the run, there would have been nothing lacking in our lives.

In January 1987 I rented a brand new luxury bus to trans-port thirty-two of my employees with me to the Superbowl in Pasadena, California. I felt I could do this because busi-ness had been good—gross sales in excess of thirty million. Christmas time I gave out bonuses to all of my eighty-four employees totalling fifty thousand dollars. But eventually my addictive gambling would screw things up again.

With the cash flow that the coupon-clearing business gen-erated, it was easy for me to juggle funds to cover my gam-bling losses. At least for a while it was. There came a time, though, when I could see that without another big-money scam I'd be in the shitter soon. So I came up with one that involved a company Lorna had worked for in Long Beach, back when we were living in Lakewood.

The company was called Apple Transit, and somehow (who can say why) I got to thinking about a time I had picked her up there in the evening. She was the only one in the office. So she had walked me over to the accountant's desk to show me how much money Apple Transit kept in its check-ing account. The total was two hundred eight-six thousand dollars, a sum memorable enough to prompt me to fly the next morning to Long Beach and rent a car.

My objective was to get my hands on a company check—a used check would be perfectly fine. And I had a plan on how to get one. I'd noticed that the company would put all outgoing mail on a table for a midday pickup in the lobby. I made a point of arriving at Apple's office about 11:20 that morning and watched the lobby from my parked car. Twenty minutes later, I saw a woman walk to a table in the lobby and place all the outgoing mail on it.

There was no one around when I slipped all the mail under my jacket and returned to my car. I drove to a mall and, while having lunch there, thumbed through the mail. A number of the envelopes contained checks. There was one for two thousand two hundred dollars made out to American Airlines and drawn on the First National Bank of Los Angeles.

I called the bank from a pay phone and told them I was from American Airlines and needed to verify whether an Apple Transit check in the amount of $103,777.09 was good. The bank said it was.

So far so good. I put all the other mail from Apple Transit in a mailbox, then xeroxed the two-thousand-two-hundred-dollar check before resealing the envelope and mailing that off too.

The First National Bank of Los Angeles was open from 9 A.M. to 1 P.M. Saturdays. After verifying that the man who endorsed checks for Apple Transit could not be reached, I phoned the bank. I told the head teller that I was Ralph Oxford, the owner of Apple Transit, and that on Friday there had been a little accident: a secretary had spilled coffee on the check-book, ruining all the checks and creating the need for new ones. The head teller said she could have a check-book sent to the company within three days. I thanked her and said goodbye, then waited an hour and called her back.

"You know," I said, "we really need a few checks right now to meet some pressing needs. I wonder if you can muster a handful for us."

"No problem," she said.

"Great. I'll send a messenger before you close."

"Tell him to ask for me," she said.

At 12:50 I arrived at the bank and said I was there to pick up an envelope for Mr. Oxford of Apple Transit.

The teller smiled: "Here you go. And would you please tell Mr. Oxford that if he doesn't receive his new checks by Thursday to please call."

"Oh sure. I'll let him know. Don't worry."

When Monday morning arrived, I opened an account at Union Bank with two hundred dollars, under the name of David Weinberg. I then deposited an Apple check into my account, made out to Weinberg for $98,300.29. I marked in the corner of the check that the check was for the purchase of land. Total bullshit. I used the xerox copy of the check made payable to American Airlines to forge Ralph Oxford's signature. Two days later the available credit in the Weinberg account was $98,500.29.

Soon after I had the bank wire ninety-eight thousand dollars to Deak Pereira—a money-changing service that had already put a hold on ninety-eight-thousand-dollars worth of gold Maple Leaf coins for me. The money eventually made it into a checking account of mine, and eased debt problems created by my gambling.

Of course the problem continued. I was burning up a lot of money. I took loans from banks that I never paid. I tried to borrow from manufacturers. And the tension was compounded by difficulties the company was now experiencing with tight profit margins. That situation was not helped either by a shady practice of some of our clients—illegal coupons.

I became acquainted with this game through a large supermarket in Oakland that would submit about five-thousand-dollars worth of coupons each week for redemption. But only some four-thousand-dollars worth of these coupons had been redeemed for the product by customers. The other one-thousand-dollars worth of coupons were clipped by the owner's family from newspapers and magazines. How did I know? Easy. If you held up all the coupons that the store submitted for, say, Fab Detergent, you could see the same cut marks on many of the coupons.

Eventually, I stopped dealing with the store. But it didn't mean an end to Pacific Clearing's problems. We owed our customers two million eight hundred thousand dollars and the manufacturers owed us three million one hundred thousand dollars. This may look good on paper, but our customers wanted to be paid pronto while the manufacturers were moving at a leisurely pace to meet our bills. Our contract with our customers obliged us to pay the supermarket chains fifteen days from the receipt of the coupons.

Well, fifteen days passed when our largest customer, the Safeway chain, ordered us to pay them in five working days or threatened to sue us. We owed them six hundred thousand dollars.

With four days left to meet that six-hundred-thousand-dollar obligation, I put an ad in the *Wall Street Journal* seeking investors. For every two hundred thousand dollars invested, I offered four percent of the business. Down to my last day, I had three investors looking over contracts with their lawyers: It looked like a done deal. So I wrote a check for the six hundred thousand dollars and FedEx'd it to Safeway, even though I only had three hundred sixty thousand dollars in the bank.

Three days later I received a call from my bank saying I did not have the funds to cover that six-hundred-thousand-dollar check. I asked the bank officer to hold the check for one day more.

"I'll be depositing four hundred thousand dollars to cover that," I said.

I fully expected that my three investors would be ready to ante up. But two of the three had a change of heart. It looked like the company was about to fold when, like the cavalry riding in to save the day, the third investor, a guy named Walter Ahrens, came through with a check for four hundred fifty thousand dollars. It was mid-afternoon, close to bank-closing time. I raced with the check to my bank and advised the officer holding the six-hundred-thousand-dollar check made out to Safeway that with Ahrens' money he could cover the check.

A close call. But I was not so naive as to think that the company was now free and clear. No way. Profit margins remained slender and my gambling excesses only aggravated the problem. So...I did what I had to do.

I opened a business called Bay Area Advertising. Bay Area Advertising did no advertising. Every Sunday five hundred San Francisco *Examiners*, two hundred San Jose *Mercury-News*, and three hundred Los Angeles *Times* were delivered to the swanky office I'd rented.

Then the group of women I'd hired would go to work, cutting the coupons in different patterns before wrinkling them and then throwing them in a garbage can. That gave the coupons a "used" look. We sometimes added in dirt for further authenticity. It added about thirty-five thousand dollars a week to the kitty.

But the bogus coupons would prove to be only a stop-gap measure. Early into 1987, we got terrible news. We were about to lose Safeway, our biggest account. Safeway generated nine-teen-million-dollars worth of income, which represented sixty-five percent of our business. Losing the Safeway account, I was convinced, would destroy us.

Why was Safeway threatening to bolt? Well, it turned out that another clearing house, formerly of Iowa and now situated in El Paso, Tex., had offered them one fifth of a penny more per coupon than we were paying. That doesn't sound significant, but you'd be surprised how that one fifth of a penny adds up. Anyway, this rival of ours could afford that largesse because while its office was in El Paso, it operated a sorting factory in Mexico, right over the border, where it paid Mexican help fifty cents an hour to sort coupons. Where we had a labor cost of two hundred forty thousand dollars a year for sorting, our rival did it for forty thousand dollars.

The logic was for us to relocate along the Mexican border. But I was against it. I was a fugitive, and it was too risky for me to be running back and forth across the Mexican border. As I owned seventy percent of the company, my opinion mattered.

But, as they say, the handwriting was on the wall. The Pacific Clearing House and Collection Agency was about to go bust. That wasn't all. There was the matter of a seventy-nine-thousand-dollar personal bank debt—a product of my lively check kiting. The bank in question felt aggrieved enough to call in the Newark, California, police. I'd even gotten a call from Newark detectives.

"We'd like you to stop by so we can see what's what with your bank problem. Okay?"

"I'd be glad to take it up with the bank," I said. "It's a bookkeeping problem, I'm told. But if necessary I'd have no problem huddling up with you folks. Let me get back to you next week and we'll schedule a sit-down, all right?"

"Next week is fine."

Fine for them. Not so fine for me.

I was worried what might happen if they fingerprinted me and found out that Fremont's pillar of society was a man-on-the-run. I rented a U-Haul, and packed it with my belongings from Fremont and Tahoe, and at midnight added in the artwork hanging on the walls of my office. I'd decided to leave behind my leased '86 silver Honda and hit the road with my leased '86 maroon Cadillac Cimmaron.

With Lorna, I was once again gone-zo.

# We got as far as Oklahoma

and I started to worry that the Cadillac might be too conspicuous. So I bought a station wagon and left the Caddy in an airport parking lot. After two days of travelling, I called Pacific and knew by our operator's voice that it was no secret any longer that I was a wanted man. I spoke to Garcia for a few minutes—long enough to sense he was already working with the feds or state police.

That was the last time I talked to Garcia, although I did call the office once more, six weeks later, only to discover they had filed Chapter 11.

In Daytona Beach, while we slept, thieves stole our U-Haul, which contained all our possessions—furniture and personal items: photos, videos, etc. That meant that when we reached our new home in North Fort Lauderdale, it was an empty house. Lorna was beside herself about it. Me? It was just a logistical problem: How do I go about getting the replacement goods?

I had two sets of ID on me at the time that the truck was stolen. I had a driver's license under the new name I was going to use in North Fort Lauderdale, which was Norman Goldman. I also still had the driver's license under the name "Weinberg" that I had been using out in California, along with several credit cards.

I had not left California broke either. I had thirty thousand dollars on deposit in a Miami bank and fifteen thousand dollars hidden in the station wagon.

Unfortunately I owed the limit on all the credit cards that I had under the name Weinberg, but I figured a way to revive the accounts. I had a fifty-thousand-dollar limit on my Visa card, on which I owed forty-nine thousand nine hundred ninety-nine dollars. So I mailed a check drawn on a closed California account and hoped Visa would credit the card before they looked into whether the check was any good. Two days later, bingo: I had fifty thousand dollars available on the Visa. I did the same with other credit cards and Lorna and I went on a one-hundred-thousand-dollar shopping spree. One hundred thousand dollars we spent in three days to fill our new ranch-style home, acquired with a twenty-thousand-dollar down payment and the owner assuming the mortgage.

Soon after moving in, in June 1987, we had our second child, a boy named Bryan. A happy event that was undercut by the humongous debt I had incurred because of my gambling. So we packed up and moved again, this time to Hoffman Estates, a fancy suburb of Chicago, where I bought a four-bedroom home for us.

I got a job with the *Chicago Sun-Times* and, on the side, started a business called United Search. I had read about a

Japanese man who had founded a business whose objective was to locate people from the distant past—a first girlfriend, a high-school buddy, so on, so forth. The article said he became a millionaire through this business.

While in Hoffman Estates, I was gambling heavily but Lorna was doing a lot worse. She'd started using drugs again, mostly freebasing cocaine. She hadn't done that in years and had promised me that if she ever took it up again I had her permission to take the kids and leave—she wouldn't be angry.

Well, I didn't know whether she meant it, really, or not. But I didn't give a hoot. The way she resisted my help, I didn't believe she'd stop. I wanted to make a life for the kids. What's more, I feared that Lorna's dealings with the drug world could bring heat that eventually would lead to my capture.

Let's be honest. Up to now I'd led a life without commitment to anything but my immediate pleasures. As it happened, those pleasures involved gambling, an experience as intense, as satisfying to me as any aphrodisiac—be it sex, drugs or power. For me, the casino was my temple, my goodtimes. Gambling was an escape of such heightened proportion that for years it had diverted me from the notion of consequences.

Oh sure, I understood that my gambling losses were the trigger for the scams I pulled and that every illegal transaction held the possibility of trouble with the law. I understood it in some distant recess of my mind and frankly, my dear, I didn't give a damn.

Or hadn't until I became a father. I'm not going to pretend that once the kids came along I became Ozzie and Harriet. Uh-uh. I'd been a selfish prick, as addictive gamblers are, for most of my adult life. Selfish and a little bent—attracted to shortcuts and shady doings from the time I was a kid. That was my nature and I didn't delude myself that I was going to become a Goody Two-shoes overnight.

But I understood that my life was on a crash course—that I had to begin to change. Change or else two sweet little children would have to bear the consequences. I didn't want any harm to come to them. I recognized that I had a problem that, if not tackled soon, was bound to become their problem.

But for now, it seemed to me that the greater threat to them was from Lorna, my common-law wife. Her use of drugs was out of hand and I had already begun to think of her as part of my past. And that had led me to take the next step and put an ad in the personal sections of the *Globe* and the *National Enquirer.*

> ILL., SWM age 35, 5'9", 150 pounds, bwn eyes, bwn hair, healthy, good sense of humor, fun loving, honest, sincere, etc. I have 2 kids, ages 6 mos and 18 mos, financially secure. No drugs.

The ad went in around Christmas time, 1987. On New Year's Eve, Lorna and I went to a party with another couple. Lorna got drunk, danced with other men, and when she refused to leave at three in the morning, I realized she had made a drug contact and had no intention of leaving with us. I got home around four, Lorna came in the following day at noon. I gave her hell. A few hours later, I stopped at my post office box in the Woodfield Mall in Shamburgh and, to my surprise, there were two hundred responses to my ad.

# The letters were from

everywhere in the States, and as close as the next town over. In my office in Elgin, I separated all the letters into piles, state by state. I spent the next six hours opening letters, reading them and looking at pictures.

I had twelve letters from the St. Louis area. I had decided to try to find a woman from that area first. Why St. Louis? Because 1) there was a race track close by, 2) it was an easy commute from Chicago and 3) it had a major league baseball team.

I placed my first call to a woman in Lake Charles, Missouri, a St. Louis suburb. I spoke with her as I looked at her picture and made a date to meet her the following week in St. Louis.

My next call was to Naomi. I had no picture of Naomi, but she wrote a nice letter and I called her anyway. She lived in an Illinois suburb of St. Louis, a small town called St. Jacob.

After talking with Naomi for about a half hour, I tried to set up a date for the following week, but Naomi insisted that next week was too long to wait, she wanted to see me that night. I explained that I was taking care of my little girl and that Lorna was taking care of my little boy and there was no way I could just hop on a plane and fly to St. Louis on the spur of the moment like that.

Three hours later I was landing at Lambert Field in St. Louis with my daughter Jeanne. I rented a car and drove out to St. Jacob. Naomi lived in an old beat-up house in a town of about two thousand. She was a tall woman, about 5-foot-11—nice looking with a pleasing figure. She told me she was a divorcee and that in the past she had worked as a cocktail waitress; at present she was selling Avon Products for a living. I told her my story, but didn't tell her I was a fugitive or that I was a compulsive gambler.

After meeting Naomi, I never bothered phoning any of the other women who had written to me. Not that I was in love with her...then or later. But I wasn't in a mood to be picky. She was good enough. I wanted someone right then and there—someone who could help raise the kids. She was just fine.

The following weekend, I gave Lorna a cock-and-bull story and flew to Orlando with Naomi. Naomi and I played cards on the flight and laughed a lot—something, I realized, I hadn't done in a long time.

The few days in Orlando—with airline tickets, motel and so forth—came to about one thousand two hundred dollars. I put it all on my American Express card. I had very little cash and, because of the gambling, I was in debt a hundred thousand dollars.

But I had a driver's license in the name of Norman Goldman and nine TRW reports on nine different Norman

Goldmans across the country. What I needed to do now was to get credit cards as these Norman Goldmans. For me cards were cash.

I took a drive around Barrington, Illinois, and made notes on homes that were under construction and nearly completed. I copied the addresses of those homes where, at the very least, a mailbox already had been installed.

I would now call banks as the first Norman Goldman and give them a change of address—using one of my "drops" in Barrington for the banks to send it to. I did that for all nine Norman Goldmans, contacting Visa, MasterCard and Discover.

I waited a week and then called all the same banks back and said, "My magnetic strip is no longer working. Could you send me a new card?"

And they did.

I had Norman Goldman credit cards up the yazoo, as well as cards in other names. Twenty, thirty cards that I converted to cash to allow me to execute my plan for leaving Lorna. Those cards gave me three hundred thousand to four hundred thousand dollars, more than enough to enable me to put down a deposit and get a mortgage for a beautiful four-bedroom home in Chesterfield, Missouri. My intention was to move into this home with Naomi and the kids.

The great escape was set up like this. I baited Lorna with a weekend in New York, so she could see her parents. She hadn't seem them in more than four years. In the past, I wouldn't allow it because her parents were not as cautious as mine. Plus, I was afraid she'd end up getting arrested and my children would be deprived of a mother.

I decided that the prospect of a trip to New York would give me the cover I needed to blow Lorna off. She and I were set to leave on a Friday. But I'd arranged for a friend from the *Sun-Times* to call while I was out and Lorna was at home. When she answered, he told her: "Please tell your husband an emergency meeting's been called at the paper for this Saturday morning. Everybody's got to be there."

She passed the message.

"Well, it doesn't matter," I told her. "You go on ahead. I'll take the kids and meet you in New York Saturday night."

"Well...I don't know," she said. "Why don't I take the kids?"

"No, that's okay," I said. "You go on up. You haven't seen your family for a while. This way you can spend time with them without having to keep tabs on the children. It's better that way. Much better."

"I don't know, Jake. I like having the kids with me."

"Don't be silly," I told her. "I'll be there later that night. We're only talkin' a part of the day."

She continued to argue that she wanted the kids, but the prospect of a big drug weekend in New York—her family was full of hardcore users—made her relent on the point eventually.

"Have a good time, honey," I said, as I saw her off at the airport.

"You hurry with the children," she said.

"No sweat," I told her.

Once she was airborne, I reconnoitered with Naomi. Naomi stayed over the house in Hoffman Estates for the night, and the following morning a moving van rolled up and began carting our stuff to Chesterfield, Missouri.

I left Lorna her clothes, jewelry, sewing machine, a thousand dollars in cash and a note reminding her of the permission she'd given me to take the kids if she went back on drugs.

"...I assume you meant what you said...when you said it—that the kids come first," I wrote, "and much as I will miss you, I have to think of the children first...You just don't seem capable at this point of getting your drug problem under control."

By the end of the day, the Jacobs' possessions had been moved to the Chesterfield home. But I decided to spend the night at Naomi's place in St. Jacob. That was Saturday. On Sunday my 800 beeper began going off like crazy. Most of the numbers were pay phones. I didn't call back. Then a number appeared that I recognized—that of friends of ours in Hoffman Estates. I called and Lorna answered.

She was crying on the phone: "I'll never use drugs again. I swear. All I have is you and the kids, Jake."

Make a long story short, she convinced me to take her back. But what was I going to tell Naomi? I honestly didn't know.

I met Lorna at a Howard Johnson's in Springfield, Illinois, and told her about Naomi...and what my plans had been before I decided to take her back. I then had her call Naomi and pretend to be from a social services agency in Chicago.

"Please tell Mr. Jacob that if he doesn't bring those two children back in forty-eight hours, there'll be a warrant for his arrest," said Lorna, pretending to be from the agency.

I drove to Naomi's home like nothing had happened. She started crying and told me this terrible news about the threat made by the social worker. With that I put the kids in the car and told her: "I'll call you."

Even though I had agreed to reconcile with Lorna, in my heart of hearts I figured she would screw up again with the drugs. When that happened, I wanted to have continuity for my children, and that was where Naomi came in. I wasn't about to tell her adios when the likelihood was that Lorna would backslide and force me to leave her for good.

But in the emotion of the moment I acted as though ours was love everlasting. I met up with Lorna and drove to

Chesterfield to show her the home that would be hers instead
of Naomi's. It was by far the biggest home we'd ever had. She
loved it.

"Oh, Jake," she said, "we're going to be so happy here. I
know it. I just know it."

"So long as you stay off the shit," I said.

"I will. I swear."

"I hope so."

"If you don't...."

"I know, Jake. I know."

"So long as you understand. I'm not foolin' around with
these kids."

"You're right, Jake. You're right."

A couple of days later, I visited Naomi and gave her the
bad news.

"I never anticipated this problem, " I said. "But the mortgage didn't go through."

"I don't understand," she said. "I thought that—"

"We don't have the house," I said. "That's the bottom line.
I thought we did, but we don't."

I told her that I'd have to move all the furniture back to
Hoffman Estates because Lorna was going to press charges
otherwise.

"This is awful, " she said.

"I agree. We'll have to finesse our way."

"Meaning what?"

"Meaning you're just gonna have to hold tight while I figure out what to do."

"Easy for you," she said.

She was right, of course. Because all this created some rad-
ical complications for Naomi. She had told her landlord she
would be moving out of her rented home by the end of the

month and had given her employer notice. I felt guilty about what I had done to her.

So I bought another house, this one for Naomi and me. This place was in Maryland Heights, Missouri. It was a smaller home, and had to be. I couldn't very well buy her a swank house after telling her I'd been turned down for the mortgage in Chesterfield. This was also a way of keeping the relationship with Naomi warm...in case Lorna lapsed.

Chesterfield and Maryland Heights were about eight miles apart, and I began to shuttle between both places, living three days a week with Naomi and the rest of the week with Lorna. When I was with one, I'd tell the other I was staying in Chicago on *Sun-Times* business. Both of them were suspicious, but neither was willing to push the matter in the beginning.

But after a while, both of them got edgier about it. Naomi cried a lot and made veiled threats about doing herself in.

"I will," she swore. "I just can't take this any more."

"Everything will be okay," I told her. "We're just in a period of transition."

"The hell we are," she said. "It's just craziness."

Lorna's anger was more smoldering, but just as scary to me. I felt tugged at and mentally exhausted. I didn't want to harm either woman, but felt that for the kids' sake I had to continue to lead the double life I was leading.

Naomi insisted we see a marriage counselor. Again there was that suicidal undercurrent in her talk. While I didn't really want to see a shrink, I figured maybe it would calm Naomi. She was a decent woman. It was worth the shot.

The marriage counselor asked me many questions while Naomi sat there and listened. One of his questions was: are you still sexually attracted to Lorna? I answered yes. I wanted to be totally truthful because I really wanted help. At the end of the session, the counselor said I belong to Lorna and not to Naomi. Just the same, I continued to see them both.

Lorna, who had been keeping to the straight and narrow, was convinced I was two-timing her and, out of anger I think, went back on drugs. Freebasing cocaine, she finally admitted, after giving me a bullshit story. When I raged at her, she agreed to separate from me so long as she could see the kids.

"Please, Jake," she pleaded. "I know I've screwed up. But if I can't see them it'll just get worse. Let me be with them and I'll try to stop the drugs."

"I've heard it before, baby," I said.

"I know. But I want to stop. Do you believe me?"

"No. You're fucked up."

"Don't say that, Jake."

"It's true."

"It's not. Just let me continue to see them."

In the end, I agreed, and got her a furnished apartment six miles from Maryland Heights. I then moved in with Naomi.

At this point I was really in bad financial shape. I owed about two hundred thousand dollars in Vegas, sixty thousand dollars to my friend Gregory and another hundred thousand on credit cards. In all, my debt was about four hundred thousand dollars. I had no money in the bank. Craving the action in Vegas, I was desperate to pay off that money.

When I got back to Chicago, I drove to my office in Elgin, where I sat around thinking about a scam I had had in mind for a long time. I had hoped, though, that I would never have to resort to it. There was a bit of risk. But with my gambling losses the way they were, I had no choice now.

At my office in Elgin, I had a Micro Bilt computer that accessed TRW. What I was about to do was run the names of a few of America's wealthiest men through the TRW computer and ask the computer to kick out credit profiles on all of them. Among my targets were the stinking-rich and sometimes famous...like Donald Trump. The others I got through *Forbes* magazine.

The fact that these were high-profile, extremely wealthy individuals made no difference to me. In fact, I'd once picked up a wallet that lay on the floor in the first-class section of an airplane and discovered it belonged to a "Willie Mays." Both Lorna and I wondered if this Willie Mays was the Hall of Fame baseball player. We decided to loiter by baggage claim and, sure enough, there was the Say Hey Kid, Willie Mays.

Lorna asked him for his autograph. Mays told her: "Don't bother me. I can't find something."

Lorna wanted me to return the wallet, but I said no. Willie was carrying two Visas, two MasterCards and an American Express card. The first place I used Willie's credit card and a phoney driver's license with his name on it was at a jai alai fronton in Tampa, where I requested five thousand dollars in cash.

"Yo, Bill, here's Willie Mays," the clerk hollered to a colleague of his.

But nobody was really suspicious. Nobody figured anybody would be crazy enough to misuse a credit card belonging to a celebrity of that magnitude. Anyway. Willie never called in the cards as stolen or lost because on a whim thirty days later, after I'd maxed all his cards, I repaid them with bad checks and used the cards all over again.

So the fact that I now was armed with credit profiles of some of America's richest men did not concern me. I had no fear of this brush with celebrity...not after the success I'd had with the great Willie Mays.

Once I had the credit profiles, I drove to Crown Point, Indiana, where I had a connection in the motor vehicle department. I met up with her at midnight and she issued licenses to me for five of my rich-guy names. In return I gave her a thousand bucks.

I then drove through Barrington again, looking as I had before for homes nearing completion. I found one that was about three months away from completion. I tore down the "For Sale" sign that was on the lawn, and then drove to Sears Roebuck, where I bought a mailbox and a label gun. Then I returned to the home and put up the mailbox. I did this with several other sites as well and then called the change of addresses for my rich guys in to the banks. A week later, I phoned again, complaining that the magnetic strip no longer worked, please send new cards.

With the credit lines these big shots had I was able to fly to Vegas and return with four-hundred-thousand-dollars worth of cash advances through the bogus credit cards. Except for the mortgage on my homes, I owed nothing.

I was now thirty-five years old and, frankly, a bit tired of the life I was leading. I had two kids I loved and was fearful of what might happen to them if I were to run afoul of the law. With Lorna troubled by drugs, it gave me a sinking feeling to think of them in a world from which I was removed.

I knew I had the wit to succeed in legit business—there was no question in my mind about that. Had I not incurred those gambling losses, my coupon-clearing business would have been a winner. Even now I was knee-deep in legit enterprises. Besides holding the newspaper job and running United Search, I had started up another business in St. Louis. "American Skiptracers" was dedicated to tracking down deadbeats...mostly for dry cleaners, supermarkets and a bank in Chicago. I got fifty percent of whatever moneys I recovered.

I was absolutely sure that if I had to I could make a legitimate living. But it meant curing my addiction to gambling and I wasn't sure I could.

For nearly thirty years, gambling had been the ultimate escape, and my scams just the means to sustain the kick. And what a kick it was. Rolling dice...betting horses...getting down on a proposition where the action is on—I was in a world of my own. All problems solved. Forgotten. I just loved the action, the excitement. It gave me a thrill every time I threw the dice. I craved wall-to-wall nonstop action. Like at the racetrack—there'd be that wait between races that made me uneasy. Couldn't stand that downtime. So I'd bring a radio and bet ballgames that I could listen to between races. That's why I always liked Vegas. When I first started going there, the sports books took action from six different race tracks. Now it's more like fifteen race tracks. You sit there and every few minutes, the horses are off and running. Nonstop action.

And the excitement is heightened by the deluxe treatment a player like me gets at the casinos. The free luxury suite. Limos. Superbowl tickets. Ladies. And late-night lunches. I didn't kid myself that giving up all that was going to be easy. I told myself, though, that now was the time to try. Really try. Time to overcome that urge for gaming action that had kept me in constant financial turmoil and felonious schemes.

It was as I anticipated changing my ways that Lorna came to me, asking to be let back into the family. She told me she had thought a lot about what she had done and how she had let us all down, and said she wanted to change. To be honest, I figured she was angling for something—I just wasn't sure what. Then she told me.

"Jake, I want to get away, far away," she said.

I frowned. What the hell was she talking about?

"You know," she said. "Somewhere remote. Secluded. Away from distractions."

"Distractions" was her way of saying drugs. That much I understood right away. What was the rest about? Well, she'd torn an advertisement from the *Sun-Times* Sunday real estate section. It was for a lakefront place in a remote part of Michigan. Cost a hundred thousand dollars. The way she saw it, this would be our home-sweet-home—a place in which she could be the mother she wanted to be to Jeanne and Bryan.

I studied the ad she put in front of me. I took a long hard look at Lorna.

"Okay," I told her. "I believe you believe what you're saying. So I'll take this last shot."

She hugged me: "You won't be sorry, Jake. I love you."

That done, I had to figure how to get the money. This time, though, no scheme jumped at me. Which was a bit unnerving. In the past, I had only to be short of money for ideas to occur. It was practically a reflex action. Like the doctor tapping his little hammer against your knee.

But my shuttling between Lorna and Naomi had been emotionally taxing. I was bushed. What had been so instinctive and easy before...suddenly wasn't. My mind was dulled, my nerves a bit frazzled. I was reluctant even to think about ways to scare up the money.

Yet I knew I'd figure something. Had to. I'd promised her this last chance. And while it was a leap of faith that probably wasn't justified, given how whacked she'd been lately, I had no other choice, really. Lorna still had that kind of hold on me.

In the midst of sorting through ideas, it occurred to me that there were unclaimed credit cards still out there—seven of them from my rich-guy scheme that I hadn't picked up yet.

With those cards, I could fly to Vegas and bang them for cash advances that would enable me to pay for the place in Michigan in cash and still have an additional fifty, sixty thousand dollars for my pocket.

Yet I was uneasy. Most business guys like to say, "Time is money." In my game, time is trouble when a scheme plays too long in one place. There was more risk here, more exposure than I cared for.

In other circumstances, I'd have said "screw it" and waited for a better idea to occur. But I wanted to believe that in this secluded place in Michigan, Lorna and I could do what we had to—begin to beat our addictions and create a more normal life for our children.

So it was that I drove to an address in Barrington and reached into the mailbox. Nothing there. I was disappointed that the box was empty, but relieved that my premonition of danger was wrong. I put down my feelings to fatigue. I needed a rest. Soon.

But first I had to get my hands on those cards. Since the mailbox was empty, I figured the post office might be holding the cards. I decided to run over there and see. I started to my car. All of a sudden a number of unmarked vehicles pulled to where I stood, their tires shrieking. Out they came—postal inspectors and secret service agents, guns drawn.

"Don't move, you son of a bitch!" one of them screamed.

I froze in place. My life on the run was over.

# CHAPTER 14

# I was arrested on May 19,

1988, and booked under the name I was using then—Jake Jacob. From prison, I phoned Lorna and had her retrieve the children from Naomi's place. I wanted the kids with their mother. I didn't really know Naomi that well.

The way Lorna and I left it was that I would call her later that night at her apartment. But when I phoned, there was no answer. I tried Naomi's place, and was more than a bit surprised when Lorna answered.

It seems that the two of them had hit it off when Lorna had picked up the kids, so Lorna had decided to stay over at Naomi's house in Maryland Heights.

When I hung up, I called my mother in New Jersey. I told her I'd been arrested and that I thought there was a good chance I could get bail.

"Come on out here," I told her. "And bring lots of money."

I needed an attorney, but didn't really know any in Chicago.

Among those being held with me in the Metropolitan Corrections Center were several inmates whose high-profile cases I'd read about in the Chicago tabloids. I figured if anybody would have proper counsel, it would be these guys. That bit of jailhouse logic led me to an attorney named Galasso.

Galasso showed up. He told me he'd need a ten-thousand-dollar retainer, and probably that would be all he'd need. I was suspicious. Ten grand seemed a bit light for first-class representation. But this was Chicago, I thought, and maybe things worked differently here. I told my mother to pay the guy. She had ten thousand dollars in an attache case, and that was how Galasso was paid. All cash.

The next time he came to see me, Galasso said, "Listen. I gotta ask ya. What's your real name?"

"Jake Jacob," I told him.

"Bullshit," he said.

"No. Really."

"I'm not buying it. 'Cause under Jake Jacob, nothin's coming back with fingerprints."

"There's no reason it should," I told him.

"Yeah. Right. And your mother's an Eskimo."

"Go fuck yourself."

Galasso came back the next day.

"If I'm gonna represent you, I gotta have your real name," he said. "I know a guy that runs as sophisticated a scam as you did is no fuckin' tenderfoot."

"I told you my name."

"You haven't told me dick."

"That's your version."

"Hey, I'm working for YOU, man."

"Then get me out of here."

"Not til I know who I have for a client."

He hammered away at me, and finally I gave in—told him my real name. Which he proceeded to give to the D.A. Which led to the authorities discovering the outstanding warrant on me back in New York. Which dated back to when I went on the lam after the law zeroed on my house in Staten Island. Which was a pretty thorough screwing when you figure I paid the son of a bitch ten grand to represent me.

Things got worse. I was refused bail. Then, when I complained to the judge that I'd been compromised by my own attorney, he told me from the bench: "You have an excellent attorney. If he gave up your name, he did it in the interest of justice."

Weird shit. Things looked bleak.

I went looking for another attorney. The new guy wanted twenty-five thousand dollars for his retainer, but he assured me he would get me off on probation...or six months sentence at the worst.

I had my mother send him a check. Once he got it, he showed up with two of his associates. And this time he was singing a different tune. He said he couldn't guarantee me that six-month sentence. It could go worse. A lot worse. Like ten years.

I walked out on him.

Then I phoned my mother and had her stop the check.

With another attorney representing me, I got thirty-two months for the credit card fraud charges and twenty-eight months for violating parole. A total of five years. As it came out in court, one of the credit card holders happened to check his available balance and discovered a change of address had been entered for him. He contacted postal inspectors, who put two and two together...and set their ambush for me.

# CHAPTER 15

# Once it became clear

I would not be granted bail, I asked my parents to take the children. I had no faith in Lorna's ability to raise them...even with the money she was making working for Citibank in St. Louis.

My parents hired a moving truck to gather my possessions from both houses and from my offices and ship them to New Jersey.

After cleaning out the Chesterfield home, the truck headed for my place in Maryland Heights, where Naomi was living. Naomi had no idea this was coming. So when Lorna started ordering the movers, "Take that couch. Take that TV," Naomi was livid. She ran to the bedroom and called the police, siccing them on Lorna.

See, when the two of them had gotten together after I was arrested, Lorna had told her there was a warrant outstanding on her in New Jersey.

Lorna was arrested and sent to the county jail in St. Louis, where postal inspectors and secret service agents interrogated her about me. Her version was that they told her if she didn't talk, I would get twenty-five years and she ten years. But if she cooperated, both of us would be out in practically no time. So she told them what they wanted to hear—gave the authorities a signed statement.

By now, with Lorna in jail, my parents had taken the children back with them to New Jersey and unloaded the truck that was full up with my possessions, even the stuff in the house in which Naomi was living. Naomi was left with only some gold, cameras and money from a bank account.

As that was happening, Lorna was being released from the county jail. From there she drove to Chicago to visit me. She never bothered to mention that she had ratted me to the feds. A couple weeks later, when her car broke down, I instructed my father to wire her five thousand dollars so she could buy a car and have some pocket money as well. As soon as she bought the car, she drove to New Jersey to live at my parents' place.

About three weeks later, I spoke to my father, who said that Lorna claimed the new car needed repairs. She was asking him for five hundred dollars. I told him to verify the details. She declined to give him any details. I knew she was back on drugs.

And soon after she was back in the joint, arrested on another warrant—not the one she mentioned to Naomi. This was an older one, for pickpocketing. She was sentenced to eight months in the Monmouth County (New Jersey) jail.

A week before she was arrested, she had taken the kids to her parents' in the Bronx, and a day's visit had lengthened into a bewildering week without contact. When we spoke by phone jail-to-jail, she admitted she'd been on drugs during that time. I conned her into granting temporary custody to my parents, persuading her that if she didn't give the kids over to my parents they would pursue legal remedies to take the kids away from her for good.

Once she granted them temporary custody, my parents filed a restraining order that stipulated she couldn't see the children until she was drug free. Well, when she finished serving her eight months, she sought relief in the court and won visitation rights. But she never did take advantage of the judge's ruling. She went right back on crack and dropped out of sight.

Meantime, I was shipped to the Federal Correctional Center in Danbury (Connecticut) to serve my time.

# CHAPTER 16

# I was in Danbury a few days

when Ray Walker tried to hide from me after I happened to spot him in the prison commissary. I knew Walker from my earlier prison stint.

I'd once lent the guy two hundred dollars and that very night he'd escaped from the joint. When I walked up to him now, he immediately spoke of squaring accounts with me.

"How much would a job in the commissary be worth to you?" he asked.

It turned out a commissary clerk was being released in thirty days. That job was worth two hundred ninety-five dollars a month, in a prison where the average inmate made a hundred fifty dollars a month working for an entity called Unicor, known to inmates as "slave labor."

Unicor produced over five hundred different items—from furniture to mailbag clips, and it made a fortune at the expense of captive labor. Inmates started at twenty-three cents an hour and eventually ascended to the grand sum of $1.25 cents an hour if their sentence was long enough.

Anyway, I agreed to forgive Walker his debt when he got me the job in the commissary.

After three months as commissary clerk, I realized the prices the institution was paying were inflated. Very inflated.

I huddled with my father and told him we could take advantage of the commissary economy.

"How?" he asked, looking puzzled.

"By forming a company that supplies goods to commissaries," I said. "All you need is a catalog and the audacity to mark up the goods one hundred percent. Which is what all these suppliers do. One hundred percent...and sometimes more. So if you pay twenty bucks for an item, you sell it for forty. We're talking sneakers, sweat suits. We're talking anything a general store would carry. Toothpaste, tooth brushes."

And so my father founded Federal Supply, made up a catalog and sent it to Danbury. The catalog landed on my desk, since my job was to order the goods that came into the commmissary.

Because Federal was a new supplier, I had to get the company's name entered into the computer. At that point I was not allowed to use the computer. My job was to type up purchase orders, delineating which supplier would provide the merchandise. Every purchase order was always rubber-stamped. Nothing was questioned. In affect, I ran things for the commissary at Danbury.

Anyway. When my father's catalog came in, I typed up a purchase order for twenty-five thousand dollars and handed it on to be signed for and entered onto the computer. At that point I spoke to the controller, showing her how Federal Supply's prices were cheaper by a lot than what we had been paying. I wanted to cover myself.

"You probably notice," I told her, "we're buying a lot of items much cheaper since I've become clerk. It's why I've added these new guys—Federal Supply."

"Jake," she said, "I don't care who you buy from. So long as you get quality items at the cheapest price."

Meanwhile, my father was working at securing merchandise at the cheapest price possible, sometimes buying in bulk on Delancey Street in New York, at other times buying from more conventional outlets. Whatever. Between me and that one hundred percent markup, the money began to roll in. Through the first five months of 1989, I was ordering forty-thousand-dollars worth of goods a month, which meant Federal Supply was taking down a twenty-thousand-dollar monthly profit.

As things developed, my job in the commissary was not only to select the suppliers but also to enter the receivables into the computer and then check the merchandise when it came off the truck. It didn't take long before I knew more about the operation than the civilian staff did. Increasingly the staff would defer to me on the particulars of the operation. Like, how to reduce prices on the merchandise. Or how to write off damaged goods. With my Macanudo cigar, I stood in the commissary all day and ran the place. In fact, I even ordered that brand of cigar, which I was partial to...and I'd take the Macanudos out of the box as if the store was mine.

In the evenings, when the commissary closed down, I'd walk two, three miles around the compound, hearing out inmate suggestions. I'd ask whether they felt prices were reasonable...what new items they wanted. I'd even hear about it if they didn't like the flavors of ice cream. I had the power to change things, and I did.

Once a week I'd give a speech to new inmates on how the commissary was run, and then engage in a question-and-answer session afterward. All other phases of prison life were addressed by staff. I was the only inmate to lecture during orientation, and that was because nobody knew as much about the commissary as I did. My position in the commissary empowered me at Danbury—from preferred housing in the honor unit to superior food. As the guy who ordered the goods, I'd add things to the purchase orders to satisfy my Jewish and Italian friends and in the process often spend dinner time in my room rather than the mess hall. What the hell. My food was better. I had cream cheese and lox on bagels, gefilte fish and horseradish, Genoa salami and provolone cheese.

As my share of Federal Supply's windfall, my parents sent one hundred dollars a month. Since I was making nearly three hundred dollars a month from my inmate job, that put me over-the-top of the prison economy. See, an inmate was limited to spending one hundred twenty-five dollars a month. But having the access I did to the computer I made it so I was able to spend as much as I wanted and rearrange spending limits for other inmates.

While Federal Supply had a good thing going, a serious complication developed. Although the revenues Federal was earning were considerable, so were the expenses involved in acquiring merchandise. What made the process a bit tricky was the lag time between billing the prison system and collecting what was due. The government was the government—slow as a snail in getting its creditors paid. But if Federal Supply was to flourish, it had no choice but to keep up with the demands of the marketplace. It couldn't suddenly retire to the sidelines and wait for the government to make good on its due bills. Either the Jacobs' organization was going to be a player, or it wasn't. But Federal Supply wasn't bankrolled by a multinational conglomerate or a J.P. Morgan. It was my ingenuity and my old man's limited capital. Eventually, push came to shove. And my parents were obliged to mortgage their house in New Jersey to keep the business going.

But I continued to do my part to give Federal every possible edge. While working in the commissary I compiled a list of the top twenty-five suppliers and rated them. Then, with the permission of Danbury's controller, I mailed out a circular with those ratings to other federal institutions. Federal Supply was top of the list. I evaluated the company as having "quality items at lowest prices, with quickest deliveries."

That certainly didn't hurt business.

A problem that did cause us some concern involved our price on a Sony digital Walkman radio. At that time, Danbury was the only institution to carry the item. My father got the radio for twenty-five dollars and his asking price was $44.95. With commissary mark-up, the price settled at fifty-seven dollars. I ordered two hundred radios and within four days was sold out. I ordered another two hundred. Well, at that point a couple of inmates discovered an ad that had the Walkman selling on the outside for $39.99. They complained about my price and the staff asked me about the discrepancy.

"They're hard to get," I said. "These guys at Federal are the only one of our suppliers that are carrying it."

That seemed to appease them. But I realized that we'd have to adjust the price on this item.

I phoned my father and told him: "You've got to make less on this particular merchandise."

"What do you want to do?" he asked.

"Take thirty-two dollars a radio."

That gave us only seven-dollar profit on each unit sold, but he agreed. That enabled me to meet the $39.99 price.

Not long after, my father and I had another conversation concerning price—this time about what to charge for L.A. Gear sneakers. When my father told me he could get the footwear for fifteen dollars a pair, we decided Federal's asking price would be $29.99. But then, when the merchandise was shipped, he discovered L.A. Gear had billed him for two hundred pairs at nine dollars a pair. So in our next phone conversation he pushed for lowering Federal's asking price to $19.99—ten dollars lower than we had discussed. But I insisted we hold to the original price. We ended up arguing heatedly about it. As it shook out, I held sway on what we would charge. At $29.99 the two hundred pairs sold out immediately.

About a month later, in January 1990, these phone conversations would bear consequences I couldn't have imagined at the time I was having them. The scenario began in the chow hall when, toward the end of dinner, an inmate named Lenny Borgi—accompanied by a friend of his—tried to bullrush me into giving up my seat so the two of them could sit there.

Borgi was a bit of a dufus—not very bright and socially inept to boot.

"Let's go, man," he said. "Get up. We want that seat."

"I'm not finished," I told him. "And you ought to learn to say 'please.' Didn't your parents teach you any manners?"

"Just give me the seat and cut the crap," said Borgi.

That's when my Italian friends began hollering at Borgi to get the hell out.

"Take your tray, and your friend, and go to the other end of the chow hall," they told him. "We don't want to see you."

You could tell that their giving him the bum's rush like that really hurt Lenny, 'cause he was Italian too...and figured that they'd back his play on account of that.

The truth is that, though I am not a particularly big guy, or a physical sort, I managed to avoid violent confrontations in both my prison stays because I was always in a position where I could do favors for people.

Running a kosher kitchen in Petersburg, and then the commissary at Danbury, gave me enough clout to make the right kind of friends. And with the right kind of friends, the predators in the prison population looked elsewhere.

That's how it was with me.

Anyway...The next day, I was sitting on a bench in front of my unit, talking with the same bunch of guys. It was a Saturday, a day off. And here comes Lenny again, settling onto a bench nearby.

I was still pissed at him for trying to show me up the day before. So I told him: "You can't sit there if I'm sitting here. Go to another unit."

He walked away with his head down and everybody laughing at him.

The next time I saw Borgi came at the end of a day that found me sitting in my room with a couple of bags of commissary goods. Borgi walked by, saw the bags and asked what was in them. I jokingly told him: "They're full of hundred dollar bills—payments from my loansharking operation."

Well, wouldn't you know? The dumb son of a bitch took it literally and immediately reported me to an associate warden.

I was locked up and put in segregation. Prison officials searched my room and found commissary inventory sheets there. I kept them in my room because I was constantly working on reorders. But they decided to base my culpability on these inventory sheets.

"They're not allowed in your room," I was told. "You've broken regulations."

I told them that staff personnel had given me the inventory sheets and were well aware that I worked on them back in my room.

"That's your story," I was told.

"It's the truth."

"The truth is you're a smartass son of a bitch and we're gonna get you, Jacob."

With that, they went and listened to all my previous phone conversations—conversations that were routinely recorded by the prison. And it was while monitoring those conversations that they heard those lengthy discussions between my father and me regarding the price of Federal Supply items—like radios and L.A. Gear sneakers. Well, it suddenly dawned on them that inmate Jacob had generated more money behind prison walls than any one of them made in salary.

They were not happy about that. And they made damn sure I would not wriggle off the hook.

They got my direct superior to lie: he denied he ever gave me permission to have the inventory sheets in my room.

A colleague of his came to visit me. He told me that he, and that superior, had been threatened with their jobs if they didn't cooperate with the prison officials in establishing a case against me.

I got confirmation of that threat from a prison guard. He said that he could pull in some favors and get me out of segregation if I wanted. But I knew it was pointless to bother. My time at Danbury had passed.

The associate warden who confronted me threw a chair at my head. It missed, but I got the general idea. I gathered that he was a bit pissed that a mere inmate (dogmeat in his view of us) had managed to screw the system once again.

"You ARE Federal Supply, Jacob," he screamed at me. "Admit it."

"Not me," I said. "It's my family that owns it."

"Bullshit. That's just a Trojan horse."

"A what?" I said, pretending not to understand his reference.

"Fuck you, you little bastard."

He paced up and back, trying without much success to calm himself. Finally, he said, "The way I figure it, you...or this Federal Supply made roughly two hundred thousand dollars from this institution. Right?"

"Sounds possible," I said.

"At least half of which is yours."

"Wrong."

"At least half," he insisted. "The minute you walk free."

"Well, set me free and I promise to tell you if you're right."

The folks at Danbury weren't about to do me that favor, or any other. They sent my ass packing to a prison in Bradford, Pennsylvania, near Pittsburgh. Shipped me with a caveat to my new jailers. This inmate is a tricky little bastard. He can steal the breeze from the trees.

In my racket, that's like a four-star rating.

# CHAPTER 17

# When I was on the run

all those years, I didn't worry much. I kind of liked the excitement...the random craziness of it all.

Sure, I was aware of the jeopardy involved, but I didn't let it overrun my emotions.

I handled the danger with a sort of professional detachment.

It was only after I was released from prison, to a halfway house in New York in June 1991, that I turned into a worrywart.

Going straight does that to you.

It wasn't for lack of money that I fretted. I was doing just fine. About a year after being released from prison, I was the owner of a thriving auction business, operating out of Linden, New Jersey, and New York City. In Linden—my main base—I worked out of a warehouse, renting four thousand square feet on which I held my auctions. Upstairs from there

I had another twenty-five hundred square feet that I used to store merchandise.

I'd stumbled onto this business while looking for a cheap car at auctions in and around the city. In the process of finding a bargain auto, I ended up with a vocation as well. I liked the excitement of the auctions—it had an accelerated pleasure not unlike gambling—and I quickly learned the intricacies of buying cheap and selling for a profit.

What you do in the auction business is buy in quantity. Say an appliance store goes belly-up. You can either acquire all the store's merchandise to resell or take a percentage of what the TVs, VCRs, and stereos go for at auction.

I caught a break when, early on, I bumped into Ron Foster, a parolee I knew from the halfway house. I had just been looking over the merchandise of a Lower East Side drugstore that was going out of business when Foster saw me out on the sidewalk. He asked me where I was coming from. The more I told Foster about my auction business, the more he wanted to invest in it.

It didn't take that much to persuade him to partner up. His cash reserves enabled us to buy large quantities of goods for auction. As Federal Auction House, we ended up grossing over two hundred thousand dollars in 1992 and made a few bucks more from a side business that Christmas.

That November, we ordered three thousand Douglas fir trees from Abraczinskas Nurseries, Inc., in Catawisse, Pennsylvania, paying seven bucks a tree or a total of twenty-one thousand dollars. We decided to sell the trees from three separate sites—one in Linden and the other two in New York City.

One of those city locations—on Canal Street and Sixth Avenue, near the Holland Tunnel—was a fenced-in lot that belonged to Mobil Oil. Once there'd been a gas station there. Now there was nothing but unused property. Foster and I knew that if we could set up our Christmas trees there, we'd do a booming business. The traffic going by was dense—one of the busiest streets in Manhattan.

But I knew that to deal with a corporate giant like Mobil would be a long, drawn-out process...and probably would not get the results I wanted. Why let a good opportunity go to waste?

I drew up a document as if Mobil Oil had leased the corner to Foster and me for the Christmas season. By the terms of this bogus paper, we agreed to pay two thousand dollars for a forty-one day lease...plus a deposit of five hundred dollars, refundable if the lot was "properly cleaned" on December 31. Then I sent in some of my workers from my auction business to break the fence locks and clean up the site.

The Christmas trees arrived the day after Thanksgiving. And so did a couple of executives from Mobil, asking what in the hell were we doing on their property. I showed them the fake document, and after looking it over they agreed that everything seemed to be in order. They jotted down the name of the nonexistent Mobil executive who was on the lease, and said they'd be in contact with me.

Well, when they couldn't locate that executive, they insisted we get liability insurance or we would have to vacate the premises. I knew a lawyer on Avenue B in the East Village. He got me instant insurance. The Mobil guys asked for a copy of the insurance for their files and that was that. We made about fifty thousand dollars profit from our Christmas trees, selling them for prices ranging from forty to eighty dollars a tree.

That was how it went for Foster and me while we were partners. We seemed to have the magic touch. Take the time we bid on a storage bin at Manhattan Mini-Storage. How this works is that when a customer stops paying for his storage space, his possessions are put up for bids—blind bids since most of the stuff is in cartons and you don't get the opportunity to sort through them. On this particular bid, Foster went there and in plain view saw a post office desk from the 1800s and guessed that the goods in the cartons would have real value. He made a bid of one thousand dollars that beat all others.

When we unpacked the stuff, we found a signed Salvador Dali painting that we had appraised for thirty-three thousand dollars. That was only the beginning. There were signed plates, silverware, all kinds of antique furniture. Something seemed out of whack. Deadbeats don't usually have stuff this pricey. It turned out that the storage company had mixed up account numbers and sold us a bin belonging to a paid-up customer, a wealthy attorney named Swanson, who did what attorneys do. He sued the storage company for big bucks.

Me and Foster? We were blameless. Foster kept the Dali. I kept some of the furniture, china and the silverware. The rest we sold. For our thousand-dollar investment we made over thirty thousand dollars on the goods we didn't keep for ourselves.

One day, Foster and I went down to the Department of Motor Vehicles in Springfield, New Jersey, so that Foster could change his Hawaiian driver's license to a New Jersey one. Well, there were one hundred fifty-five people—we counted the bodies—and an interminable wait ahead of us. As we scoped out the situation, it occurred to us that we would pay so as not to have to wait hours to get a license. Would other folks do the same? We asked the people standing in line. Enough of them said yes to inspire our next business venture: DMV Express, Inc.

For twenty-nine dollars, you would drop off your papers and DMV would process them so that you could avoid all the waiting. In time, DMV would process not just individual applications but the paperwork for fleets of automobiles—from car rental companies and other businesses. DMV became a going enterprise.

And so was I. But what should have been a time for celebration was not. My life was being undermined by a battle between my parents and me for custody of the children. It was rooted in their unhappiness about my relationship with a woman named Mary, who was Jamaican and black.

My mother offered to move the children and me to Israel and set me up in a business there if I told Mary goodbye. Later, she offered to buy me a home in Union, New Jersey—again on the condition that I dump Mary.

When I refused her offer, she cut off all credit cards and stopped giving me money. That was okay. I could make money on my own. But their bitterness about Mary intensified when Mary and I married on April 23, 1992, and it drew us into a long and costly battle for custody of the children.

Their decision to challenge me for custody of the children—they'd had temporary custody while I was in prison—marked the beginning of troubling complications that went beyond the lunacy of court proceedings. For in their resolve to get control of the children, my parents were bent on nothing less than ruining me.

For instance, when my probation officer shook hands with me in August 1992, he was saying goodbye and good luck—I'd finished probation. But when my parents found out that I'd been given a foreshortened probation—the court in Chicago did not view me, apparently, as a major threat to society—they agitated to have my probation reinstated.

On July 21, 1993, they succeeded. That was the date of a letter I received from the probation office of the United States District Court in Newark. The message was that not only was I back on probation but that I was to show proofs of having made payments toward the restitution of $200,009.65 that the court had ordered on February 15, 1989, when I was sentenced on mail fraud and credit card fraud in Chicago.

Thomas J. Stone was the probation officer I was ordered to meet on August 4 in Newark. When I did, he acted like a pawn of my parents, even using language that parroted words they had constantly used in court. Saying, for instance, I was not a credible person—I lied all the time. That was straight out of their mouths. When I asked him had he spoken to my parents, Stone replied, "I ask the questions, not you."

Stone then ordered me to sell my New York business, sell my cars and withdraw all the money I had in the bank and give it to him as restitution payment. I called my old parole officer from Brooklyn and told him what had happened. He checked things out and discovered that I had not yet officially been put on Stone's case load.

"Get back to New York and you'll be okay," he told me.

Soon after, I moved from New Jersey to Queens. When I looked up my old parole officer, I assumed I would be under his control...only to discover that my current address was out of his jurisdiction.

"But don't worry," he said. "There's nobody like Stone in the system here."

He gave me the name of the man I'd report to and assured me there'd be none of the chickenshit with him. That was the impression I had when, a few days later, I met the guy. But seconds after we had shaken hands, his phone rang and when he hung up, he turned to me and said: "I'm not going to be your probation officer."

The new probation officer was Darcy A. Zavatsky, a young, attractive woman whose objectives, it quickly became clear, were punitive. She advised me that she expected me to pay eight thousand two hundred dollars a month restitution, and to advise the New Jersey Department of Motor Vehicles that I was an ex-convict, which would have killed DMV had I paid heed to her. And like Stone, she planned to institute other measures to squelch my economic initiative and potential, including but not limited to successfully forcing me to sever my business relationship with Foster.

On November 5, 1993, my attorney, Robert Blossner, wrote Zavatsky the following:

> Dear Ms. Zavatsky:
> Although you did not return my call or respond to my letter of October 28th, I have received a copy of your letter to Mr. Jacob of November 2nd in which you direct him to pay $8,200 per month toward restitution. Please be advised that Mr. Jacob is physically, financially and emotionally unable to make such payments. As you are well aware, he is in the midst of litigation concerning the custody of his children, whom he lost when he was incarcerated. He is also desperately trying to establish his company during the midst of the economic recession. Of course, he must also make provisions for the payment of federal and state income and business taxes out of his monthly income. Your demand of $8,200 per month is so far "beyond the pale" that even an attempt to satisfy it would render his efforts to reenter societies mainstream devastated. He would definitely lose his children, probably his business and incur a tax lien that could realistically never be satisfied. If you are adamant in your demand and inflexible as to

> adjusting the amount, I can see no other alter-
> native but that you seek a violation hearing
> before Judge Duff who imposed Mr. Jacob's
> sentence.

The way I doped it out, Newark (and Stone) had influenced the change of probation officer, siccing Zavatsky on
me. Hardhearted Darcy. She seemed genuinely galled by my
business success, particularly the material symbols of
it...which I would discover were far grander than what she
could boast.

I had a bunch of credit cards, with limits of up to twenty
thousand dollars. She had only one card, with a thousand-
dollar cap. I owned a '94 Olds, a '93 Grand Am, a couple of
vans and a Dodge station wagon. She allowed as how she had
only one car, a 1986 sedan.

She made a point of comparing her economic stability—
she owed not a dime, whereas I owed more than two hundred thousand dollars in restitution—and resented that I was
leading the life of Riley. A convicted criminal ought to know
his place.

As I say, I found myself constantly worrying. Worrying
about what Zavatsky might try to screw me up. Worrying
about whether I would gain custody of my kids. Worrying
how to pick up the financial slack that the loss of Foster
occasioned.

I had the feeling that my past was an incitement for a pay-
back—that the sort of white-collar angles player I'd been was
an affront to others, and now that they had me as a stationary
target, they didn't mind sticking it to me. By early 1994, the
court had ruled against me, awarding my parents custody of
my children and me weekend visitation rights. The lies and
bullshit my parents had put forth in the courtroom were swal-
lowed whole. Meanwhile, Zavatsky persisted in doing what

she could to hamstring my financial progress. So rather than remain an opportune target for her, I declared bankruptcy in May 1994. By that act, I hoped to make restitution a dead issue and squelch my probation officer's excessive interest in my case. Whether my declaration of bankruptcy accomplishes that remains to be seen. My attorney contends that bankruptcy will remove the restitution burden. Zavatsky is arguing that it does not. A bankruptcy court will ultimately decide.

These are hard times, but I've always had the ability for bouncing back. And I expect I will again. Still, there are days when I feel like I'm walking uphill with a hundred pound weight on my back. Not that I expect anybody to feel sorry for me. Guys like me don't usually generate a whole lot of sympathy. Folks prefer their antisocial sorts to learn from their experience...and change. Twenty years is a long time to have done what I did. Over those two decades I was steadfast in purpose. Find a loophole in the business fabric and work it until the money ran dry.

So I can understand it if there's not a whole lot of sympathy for Jake. You want to dance—the fiddler must be paid. By the same token, while I do my damnedest now to walk the straight and narrow, I don't feel the urge to prostrate myself before society for its forgiveness. I did what I did, and I paid for it. And still am. So if you're looking for a bouquet of regrets and mea culpas, sorry—you've come to the wrong place. If I changed, it was to be a father to my children. And with any luck, when my appeal is heard, I'll have custody again.

In the meantime, I don't feel compelled to recant my past or do acts of contrition.

I had a knack. I could look at the everyday routines of commerce and, like-that, know how to exploit them. I made a ton of money and had me an adventure.

It's not a bad parlay.

# In January 1995,

in a federal court in Brooklyn, Craig Jacob was found guilty of violating his probation and sentenced to a seven-and-a-half-year prison term. Authorities accused Jacob of check fraud in West Virginia and New Jersey. Jacob denied the charges and intended to appeal his probation violation.

# The Jacob Papers: An Addendum

The language in the court documents has not been altered.

# July 31, 1981

The following is an excerpt from a pre-sentencing report about Craig Barry Jacob, dated July 31, 1981

The defendant has been examined by psychiatrists and psychologists since 1970, in view of his addiction to gambling and his entanglements with the law. The 1972 District of New Jersey pre-sentence report notes the results of two examinations. A report prepared at the Diagnostic Center in Menlo Park, New Jersey, in November, 1970, describes the defendant as schizoid, and as having deep feelings of inadequacy with aggressive and unrealistic over-compensatory needs. Another report, prepared in July, 1971, by Dr. Howard Schartz in Maplewood, New Jersey, reflects that the defendant suffers from a sociopathic personality disturbance manifested by compulsive gambling and antisocial behavior.

In July, 1972, Doctor Sheldon Rogers conducted an evaluation of the defendant at the federal facility in Ashland, Kentucky. The report described the defendant as having superior intelligence, but as suffering from a sociopathic personality disorder.

The psychiatrist believed that the defendant had the innate intelligence to benefit from individual psychotherapy, and that, in fact, therapy would be a more appropriate form of treatment for him rather than his membership in Gamblers Anonymous.

The defendant impressed this officer as an intelligent individual, who attempts to minimize and excuse his many crimes over the years, laying the blame on his activity on his uncontrollable blame for gamble. However, during the interviews, he expressed no remorse for any of his actions, nor did he express any desire to involve himself in any type of program which could extricate him from the monotonous routine of gambling and fraud his life has been over the past eleven years. In sum, this defendant appears to be an individual for whom fraud and criminal activity have become a way of life, and who shows no sign of wanting to change.

Financial Status. The defendant has no assets. He claims that he has paid off $20,000 in gambling debts. However, in order to pay these debts, he had to take out cash advances from American Express and from Master Charge. He owes $12,000 to American Express and $2,000 to Master Charge.

EVALUATION:
The defendant, now 28 years old, has been a compulsive gambler since his adolescence, and has obtained the funds to satisfy that addiction by victimizing his own parents and many others through fraudulent activity. While he appears to have gone through the motions of seeking assistance by joining Gamblers Anonymous, his sporadic and half-

hearted cooperation with that program indicates that he has little motivation to gain control over his life. Following his 1972 conviction on federal charges, the defendant received benefit of a Youth Correction Act sentence and was released from after two years. While he did work and report regularly for parole supervision, he was arrested five times during that period, of which two have resulted in this conviction and one other federal conviction. As a result of his commission of the instant offense, the employer he defrauded, a trucking company, lost its largest account, a loss which contributed at least in part to the closing of the firm. In addition, his failure to appear in this Court and in the Southern District of New York led to a judgement against his parents and financial loss to them. Whether the defendant's gambling addiction can be pinpointed as the sole root of his criminal activity, it is certain that he has an uncontrollable urge to defraud. His sentence to a period of incarceration appears necessary to protect society from his criminal behavior. In addition, however, it may also afford him an opportunity, within an appropriate setting, to establish some control over his pathology and criminal tendencies.

RESPECTFULLY SUBMITTED:
JAMES F. HARAN
CHIEF U.S. PROBATION OFFICER
Prepared by: (signed) Paul M. Visokay
Approved by: Irene (signature of last name
            indecipherable)

United Search, Inc.
339 West River Road
Elgin, IL 60120
(312) 695-2211

*We find needles in hay stacks.*

01/13/88

TRW
Marketing Dept.
1699 Wall Street
Mt. Prospect, Il. 60056

Marketing Dept:

I would like to become a subscriber to your service. Our
firm works directly with banks and finance companies, to
locate skips.

We will also need a terminal, which I was told, you
could supply. We plan to pull up approximately 20-50
reports per month. Presently we have access to your reports
thru First Chicago Bank, but this is a great inconvience.

Please send us all the necessary paper work to be filled
out.

Sincerely,

John Jacobs

JJ:lkt

1699 Wall Street
Mt. Prospect, IL 60056
312.931.9400

February 15, 1988

Mr. Jake Jacobs
United Search Inc.
338 West River Road
Elgin, IL 60120

Dear Mr. Jacobs,

**WELCOME AND THANK YOU** for the privilege of serving your credit information needs. The enclosed copy of your service agreement is for your records and your Account Executive will contact you shortly to arrange a training.

Listed below is your subscriber identification code number. The last three or four digits, your password, are a unique alpha numeric security code that is yours alone. Only inquiries entering the system with your subscriber code number and security password will be billed to your company.

### 2980053 PASSWORD BØM CONTROL OYN

BECAUSE OF THE PROPRIETARY NATURE OF THE DATA BASE, WE MUST REQUEST THAT YOU AND YOUR EMPLOYEES MAINTAIN YOUR CODE NUMBER/PASSWORD UNDER THE STRICTEST SECURITY.

If, at any time, you have questions regarding our services, please do not hesitate to call our Customer Service Department at 312/981-9400. We're proud to serve you!

Very truly yours,

Regional Director
Midwest Region

# June 5, 1988

File number 3-201-771-112160-5
A statement given by Jacob's common-law wife, "Lorna
Simmons," to Special Agent Richard Alto on June 5, 1988.

"...In 1982, I met Jake Jacob, AKA Craig Barry
Jacob, in Bronx, N.Y.,and cashed stolen checks for
Jacob at 15-20 banks in Pennsylvania until I was
arrested by local police. Jacob had a stack of
blank NY driver's licenses which we used to assume
numerous identities and to gain credit cards, cash
advances, bank loans, open checking accounts and
cash stolen checks. I used the following names in
this scheme: Denise Del Vechio, Sydnee Goldman,
Sydnee Goodman, Sydnee Otner and Sydnee Jacob.
Craig Jacob used Jake Jacob, Norman Goodman, David
Weinsteen, Norman Goldman, Norman Gellman, Melvin
Blitzstein, Donald Trump. Since Jacob and I were
both fugitives, we used the above alias names and
traveled to Tampa, Fla.; Lakewood, Ca.; Fremont,
Ca; Plantation, Fla; West Palm Beach, Fla.; Hoffman
Estates, Ill. and Chesterfield, Mo....Jacob and I
routinely applied for and obtained credit cards as
a result of mailing fraudulent credit card appli-

cations to numerous credit card companies....At
each location we moved to we would use the money
obtained from the use of the fraudulently obtained
credit cards to support gambling habits and to pay
for living expenses.

# November, 1988

From the pre-sentencing report of Susan Rozanski, U.S. Probation Officer, regarding Craig Barry Jacob (Docket No. 88, CR 426-1) Nov. 1988.

PERSONAL AND FAMILY HISTORY

The following information was gathered orally from the defendant and corroborated by information culled from his previously prepared pre-sentence report of 1981. It was verified that Craig Barry Jacob was born on Feb. 3, 1953 to Arnold and Jeanne Jacob (nee Barnett) in Newark, New Jersey. He is the oldest of three children born to this inact marital union. Mr. Jacob recalled that he was reared in an upper middle-class lifestyle as his grandparents were wealthy from their furniture business and his father was a mechanical engineer for Wagner Electric. He related that most of the students in his peer group were the offspring of millionaires. He gambled in high school, going to the racetrack everyday. When asked what his parents thought of this behavior, he responded that his parents generally went along with whatever he wanted-ed. The following is an excerpt prepared by United

States Probation Officer Kenneth B. Greenblatt in August 1981.

"He was friendly with sons of a number of millionaires during his high school years. This apparently is one explanation for his compulsive gambling, as it allowed for possible successful financial gains while still young and later became a compulsive habit difficult to break.

"During most of his childhood years, the defendant grew up in his parents' home located at 134 Valley View Road, Hillside, New Jersey, a one-family dwelling described as being in a good residential neighborhood with the home being in excellent physical condition. Although the defendant has moved around the United States frequently and has had his own apartments in New Jersey and New York City, he apparently has close ties to the family as he frequently contacts them for their assistance when in any legal difficulties.

"It is interesting to note that previous reports suggest inconsistent discipline on the part of his parents with the mother being highly protective and given to rationalizing his behavior while the father has been frustrated in his attempts to set standards and to discipline the defendant. The mother previously suggested that her son committed the offense of Transportation of Stolen Securities in Newark, New Jersey, so as to support his compulsive gambling. She was of the opinion at that time that Gamblers Anonymous would be sufficient in changing her son's lifestyle and illegal behavior. The mother has again been interviewed and questioned about the instant offense. Interesting enough, she is fully supportive of her son believing once again his gambling habits interfered with his ability to remain law-abiding, and she considers the problem to be a disease much like cancer. She explained that it is important for her to provide both the emotional and financial support necessary for her son as anyone would in treating a family member afflicted with cancer. She further explained that her son has now "reached rock bottom" and as a result he can go no further downward and is most definitely now on the road to recovery. Mrs. Jacob went on to explain that her son would most definitely benefit from attending Gamblers Anonymous as he has no choice now but to be motivated in that direction.

"When the father was interviewed by another probation officer, he presented much the same bleak picture as he had previously done during an earlier interview done some years ago. He believes his son to have been pampered and his wife providing too much support which the son takes advantage of. Due to legal fees and other financial responsibilities resulting from their son's criminal endeavors, they are no longer in a position to provide for him, especially in regard to legal fees. This has been a cause of much stress in the immediate family."

Mr. Jacob related to the undersigned writer that after his release in 1982, he used a stolen credit card and moved to Florida. He indicated that he lived in Tampa for three months and essentially has been "on the lam" for the past four years. He opened his own business known as Allstate Trading which

bought secondhand merchandise for resale. He did
this for approximately six months. He stated that
he used to go to Las Vegas every weekend and gambled at the racetrack as well as with bookmakers.
He stated that he took $30,000 to $40,000 from
banks. He indicated that his paramour worked for
Kelly Girl and she stole checks from the offices
where she worked. He states that they were never
indicted on these charges. He admits to using a
number of aliases, including Norman Goldman, Norman
Gellman, and that he was able to get a driver's
license and credit card under these names. He
states that he owes money on various credit cards
and that he kept detailed records in hopes of paying all of his creditors back. He moved to Fremont,
California, in September 1985, and opened a business known as Northwest Retailors. This was a
clearing house for coupons from department stores.
He indicated that about this time he started losing heavily at the racetrack and that he moved from
Alameda County to Florida in 1986. He states that
he paid taxes under the name of Norman Goldman. He
indicated that his business was listed in Dunn and
Bradstreet. He indicated that in 1986, he moved to
Hoffman Estates and opened a business in Elgin,
Illinois, called United Search. He states that the
function of this business was to locate outstanding debtors. He used the name of Norman Goldman. he
states that he would take his credit cards to Las
Vegas and gamble up to amounts of $500,000.

On the advice of attorneys, a section from this pre-sentencing
report, entitled "Parents and Siblings," has been deleted.

MARITAL

The defendant states that he has never been married. He reports a cohabiting relationship with "Lorna Simmons," age 33. He states that he met her in jail in Monmouth County, New Jersey.* She has currently been in custody for two months and she is serving an eighteen month custody sentence for distribution of a controlled substance. The defendant related that she freebases cocaine. He related that his parents have legal custody of the couple's two children. They are Jeanne Marie, born April 18, 1986, and Bryan Harry born June 5, 1987. He indicates that he talks to the children on a regular basis and has had recent physical contact with them. The defendant's mother confirmed these dates of birth and the fact that she provides support for the children.

The 1981 pre-sentence report reflects that the defendant lived with a "Helen Stevens" at 350 East 62nd Street in New York City for approximately six months. He and Helen Stevens met when they were both serving federal sentences. The report reflected that the defendant visited Helen Stevens when she was out on furlough in August 1974, and apparently he was in violation of his condition of parole at that time. The defendant provided little information as to the relationship he had with Ms. Stevens except to accuse her of informing the FBI as to his whereabouts which led to his arrest. The defendant's mother, Mrs. Jacob, was interviewed and she blamed Ms. Stevens for her son's downfall as

---

*Jacob claims this account of their first meeting is factually in error.

she claimed he was making a better adjustment in the community before the two began living together. It was Mrs. Jacob's belief that Ms. Stevens was a drug addict in need of illicit drugs and lived expensively which resulted in her son's continual need for additional funds. It was noted however, that she could provide no substantial evidence of this claim.

EDUCATION

Records reviewed by the previous pre-sentence report reflected that the defendant attended Hillside, New Jersey, public schools, but failed to graduate in his senior year of high school. Mr. Jacob's account was that he missed too many days as he was at the racetrack. He reports that he attended the University of West Virginia in Morgantown from 1971 to 1973, and the University of New York (NYU) in Manhattan, from 1974 to 1976 (verified).

EMPLOYMENT

March 1988 to May 1988 (2 months) (unverified)

The defendant reports that he had his own company known as American Skip Trace. This self-employed venture was designed to locate people who were "skips" for credit card companies. He states that he was doing this when he was arrested.

1988 (5 months) (unverified)

The defendant reports that he formed his own company known as Federal Consultants. This company allegedly worked with federal prisoners to facilitate them gettting transfers within the Bureau of Prisons systems and to work on "small legal problems." The defendant reports that he earned $20,000 annually. His supervision file from New Jersey contains copies of checks drawn on the Federal Consultants bank account located at 88 8th Avenue, Suite 1102, New York City, New York. The checks are signed by his mother, Jeanne Jacob.

1981 to 1983 (2 years) (verified)

The defendant was incarcerated as a result of his previously imposed federal sentences.

It should be noted that the defendant's work history was difficult to verify because of his many self-employed ventures and use of aliases, and frequent change of address. Mr. Jacob's previously-prepared pre-sentence report reflects that between 1971 and 1972, he held various jobs in the field of bookkeeping and accounting. One firm, the Consolidated Sewing Machine Company in New York City brought charges against him because of his embezzling business funds. It is this case that the warrant in Manhattan Criminal Court remains outstanding for his failure to appear on a violation of probation hearing due to not making restitution payments. Records indicate that an advertising firm, Salters & Sabinson, also in New York City, discharged the defendant when an audit discovered certain irregularities. Jacob was accused of issuing checks to some of the firm's California employees, forged the name and uttered them.

When released on parole, Mr. Jacob began working part-time for Ace Inventory Company in the Bronx earning $3 an hour. Between 1974 and 1976, he worked full-time for Champion Envelope Company in

Brooklyn earning $350 per week as an inventory and production analyst. In 1976, Jacob worked as an assistant manager for Avante Lauren Company, and in 1977 at Arrow Trucking Company in Jersey City. It was then that Jacob began his own business known as World Wide Distributors, which has been described by the Eastern District of New York to have been a fencing operation for stolen goods.

## MILITARY SERVICE

The defendant has never served in the United States Military.

## HEALTH

Physical: The defendant is a Caucasian male who stands 5'9" tall, weighs 150 pounds and has brown eyes and brown hair. He states that he has never been hospitalized nor undergone any type of surgery. He describes his health as good. He is currently taking Acutane to promote his skin healing. He states that he does not drink alcohol, but has used cocaine and marijuana. He denies ever using it on any regular consistent basis. He smokes cigars.

Mental and Emotional: During the preparation of this report, Mr. Jacob indicated that he was seeking professional help from the Forensic Center for Compulsive Gambling. He stated that he was evaluated by Valerie C. Lorenz, Ph.D. Mr. Walsh, defense counsel, indicated that he would forward this evaluation.

Progress reports prepared by the Federal Correctional Institution located in Danbury, Connecticut, reflect that Mr. Jacob made an average institutional adjustment. He had incurred two misconduct reports in November 1981, at the New York Metropolitan Correctional Center, involving an unexcused absence, lying, and being in an unauthorized area for which 40 hours of extra duty was ordered in addition to a job change. On July 30, 1982, at the Federal Correctional Institution at Raybrook, New York, Mr. Jacob was charged with possession of an unauthorized tool, possession of a narcotic and possession of gambling paraphernalia. The Internal Disciplinary Committee at Raybrook confiscated the contraband, gambling slips and one blue nitrostat pill and awarded ten extra hours of duty. At that time, in 1983, the progress report indicated that Mr. Jacob was a viable, active participant in their Gamblers Anonymous program.

Although there are no substantiating intelligence test scores available, Mr.Jacob impressed the undersigned writer as a man of above-average and possibly high intelligence. He is the type of person who, equipped with almost little or no information, can make optimum use of it and obtain mobility in spheres that would present barriers to most of us who are not willing to persist or who lack tenacity. He is not intimidated easily, nor is he afraid to test limits.

There is no question that he is obsessed by the need for money and the power which it wields. What is particularly unfortunate in Mr. Jacob's case is that he probably possess the skills and talent to make a profitable and lucrative income through legitimate channels. There also seems to be little question that he is afflicted with gambling as a disease as most alcoholics are with drinking. Gamblers Anonymous and incarceration have not however acted as significant deterrents or controls for Mr. Jacob. Although Mr. Jacob has admitted his illegal behavior, he appears devoid of any regret or recognition of its seriousness or impact.

He recognizes that his mother is the best equipped provider at this point for his children. One questions what kind of life the two toddlers must have had with parents who had cocaine and gambling addictions, and who were constantly "on the run."

FINANCIAL

| | |
|---|---|
| Assets: | $0.00 |
| Cash | $0.00 |
| Unencumbered Assets | $0.00 |
| Equity in Other Assets | $0.00 |
| TOTAL ASSETS | $0.00 |

| | |
|---|---|
| Unsecured debts | |
| Various credit cards | $200,000.00 |
| Mother, Jeanne Jacob | $300,000.00 |
| TOTAL UNSECURED DEBTS | $500,000.00 |

EVALUATION

Mr. Jacob is every credit card holder's nightmare. This man has single-handedly developed a sophisticated scheme that puts banks with all their modern state of the art computer equipment at his mercy. He not only falsely represented his identitites to such large corporations as Visa and Discover Cards, but he also contacts individual credit card holders instructing them to destroy their credit cards.

He used these credit cards to lead a lifestyle that subsidized luxuries and his gambling compulsion. He used worthless checks to pay fraudulently-obtained credit card bills.

A recurrent reason given for the defendant's illegal behavior is his gambling disease. There is no dispute over the fact that Mr. Jacob gambles with the ease with which most people breath. He somehow feels that it is this court's responsibility to cure him of this disease or to be lenient with him because of his gambling disease in its sentence. Mr. Jacobs has been engaged in gambling behavior since the age of seventeen. He has shown virtually no signs of decreasing this activity no matter what the imposed consequence was. He has been sentenced under the Youth Corrections Act, he has served time on four separate indictments, and all his behavior in between reflects repeated, unceasing, fraudulent activity.

If the court were to consider that Mr. Jacob's gambling disease follows a medical model like alcoholism, then a reasonable conclusion would be if his gambling cannot be cured like many alcoholics cannot be "cured," then its negative effects and symptoms must be controlled. He cannot be allowed to continue committing crime simply because he has a disease, which he cannot cure or contain. Since he cannot control his disease, steps must be taken to limit its illegal and disasterous consequences on society. If Mr. Jacob had an incurable organic brain syndrome and was hurting or killing people, we would not be inclined to be more lenient with him at the risk of jeopardizing the safety of the community.

FEDERAL CORRECTIONAL INSTITUTION
DANBURY CT 06811-3099

NO. 0529

| APPR | BA | COST CENTER | PMS | PROJ | SUB OBJECT | IQ | DOC TYPE | PURCHASE ORDER NO | DESQ | DESQ | |
|------|----|----|-----|------|------------|----|----------|-------------------|------|------|--|
| X4 | 1 | 323 | 536 | CMS | 2670 | N | 05 | 0410 | CMS | CFS | N |

ALL INVOICES SHALL BEAR THE ORDER NUMBER AND BE SUBMITTED IN DUPLICATE

FEDERAL SUPPLY
PO BOX 2687
ELIZABETH N.J. 07207

CONSIGNEE AND DESTINATION
FEDERAL CORRECTIONAL INSTITUTION
RTE 37
DANBURY CT 06811-3099
REFER TO PO#

ATION NO Hatley  CONTRACT NO. O/N

TIME FOR DELIVERY 3/22/90

DISCOUNT TERMS NET 30

DESTINATION ORIGIN  XXDURXXXXX MEM.

| ARTICLES OR SERVICES | | | QUANTITY | UNIT | UNIT PRICE | AMOUNT |
|---|---|---|---|---|---|---|
| 0111111175 | 06-01 LaGear Sneaker | Size 7½ | 3 | pr | 39.00 | 117.00 |
| 0111111180 | 06-01 LaGear Sneaker | " 8 | 8 | pr | 39.00 | 312.00 |
| 0111111185 | 06-01 LaGear Sneaker | " 8½ | 8 | pr | 39.00 | 312.00 |
| 0111111119 | 06-01 LaGear Sneaker | " 9 | 4 | pr | 39.00 | 156.00 |
| 0111111195 | 06-00 LaGear Sneakers | " 9½ | 5 | pr | 39.00 | 195.00 |
| 0111111110 | 06-01 LaGear Sneaker | " 10 | 4 | pr | 39.00 | 156.00 |
| 0111111105 | 06-01 LaGear Sneaker | " 10½ | 4 | pr | 39.00 | 156.00 |
| 0111111111 | 06-01 LaGear Sneaker | " 11 | 6 | pr | 39.00 | 234.00 |
| 0111111115 | 06-01 LaGear Sneaker | " 11½ | 3 | pr | 39.00 | 117.00 |
| 0111111112 | 06-01 LaGear Sneaker | " 12 | 3 | pr | 39.00 | 117.00 |
| 0411111175 | 06-04 Head Sneaker | Black " 7½ | 3 | pr | 29.00 | 87.00 |
| 0411111118 | 06-04 Head Sneaker | " " 8 | 8 | pr | 29.00 | 232.00 |
| 0411111185 | 06-04 Head Sneaker | " " 8½ | 8 | pr | 29.00 | 232.00 |
| 0411111119 | 06-04 Head Sneaker | " " 9 | 4 | pr | 29.00 | 116.00 |
| 0411111195 | 06-04 Head Sneaker | " " 9½ | 5 | pr | 29.00 | 145.00 |
| 0411111110 | 06-04 Head Sneaker | " " 10 | 4 | pr | 29.00 | 116.00 |
| 0411111105 | 06-04 Head Sneaker | " " 10½ | 4 | pr | 29.00 | 116.00 |
| 0411111111 | 06-04 Head Sneaker | " " 11 | 6 | pr | 29.00 | 174.00 |
| 0411111115 | 06-04 Head Sneaker | " " 11½ | 3 | pr | 29.00 | 87.00 |
| 0411111112 | 06-04 Head Sneaker | " " 12 | 3 | pr | 29.00 | 87.00 |
| 1222222123 | 4214S LCD Watch Mens | | 300 | ea | 1.25 | 375.00 |
| 131971627 | GE Walkman Radio | | 120 | ea | 19.95 | 2394.00 |
| 163108320 | 11-05 Headphone Nura | | 60 | ea | 6.30 | 378.00 |

DO NOT TYPE IN THIS SPACE

TOTAL 8221.00

NOTE: See Terms and Conditions on Reverse
NOTE: IF THIS ORDER IS F.O.B. SHIPPING POINT, SHIP PREPAID VIA CHEAPEST AVAILABLE MEANS. TRANSPORTATION CHARGES TO BE INCLUDED ON INVOICE AS A SEPARATE ITEM WHICH SHALL BE SUPPORTED BY ORIGINAL FREIGHT BILL OR EXPRESS BILL. DO NOT INSURE PARCEL POST SHIPMENTS.
DELIVERY HOURS: 8 A.M. TO 3 P.M. LOCAL TIME
Except Saturday, Sundays and Government Holidays.

SIGNATURE Mary Moerler

PROCUREMENT OFFICER 3/8/90
Mary Moerler 203-743-6471 ext 404
Questions concerning payment should be directed to John Gonzalez Accounting Supervisor ext 411

VENDOR

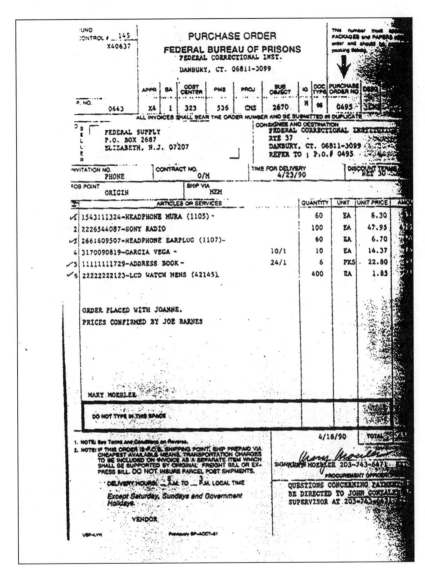

PURCHASE ORDER

FEDERAL BUREAU OF PRISONS
FEDERAL CORRECTIONAL INST.
DANBURY, CT. 06811-3099

ORDER PLACED WITH JOANNE.
PRICES CONFIRMED BY JOE BARNES

MARY MOERLER

**ABRACZINSKAS NURSERIES, INC.**
Triple A Quality - Over 70 Years

SEEDLINGS
TRANSPLANTS
NURSERY STOCK
CHRISTMAS TREES
RELATED PRODUCTS
:VER TO:
Canal Street
Ave & Canal
York, NY
-229-9806

R.D. #1, Box 6
Catawissa, PA 17820

FAX — 717-366-2366
Office — 717-356-2323

Federal Auction House
824 East ST George Ave
Linden, NJ  07036
908-486-4074
212-851-5446 Craig Jacob - Beeper

November 17 ___ 19 92

| Quantity | Size | | | | | |
|---|---|---|---|---|---|---|
| | | 1992 CUT CHRISTMAS TREES | | | | |
| | | | | | | |
| 3000 | | Douglas Fir | 7 | 00 | 21000. | 00 |
| | | | | | | |
| | | | | | | |
| | | The above price is delivered. | | | | |
| | | 25% deposit to confirm order. | | | | |
| | | Balance due on delivery | | | | |
| | | | | | | |
| | | Delivery Date: 1st load Nov 26  7am | | | | |
| | | Will let us know on next delivery dates | | | | |
| | | | | | | |
| | | | | | | |
| | | Information for wiring deposit: | | | | |
| | | Bank # 031308315  Liberty Bank, Mt Carmel, PA | | | | |
| | | Checking account # 8800-803-0 | | | | |

Sublease Agreement entered into this 15th day of November , 1992 between

DMV EXPRESS, INC.         , (Tenant) and
Marvin Miller            : (Subtenant) and
Mobil Oil, Co.           (Landlord).

Sublease Period: The Subtenant agrees to sublease from Tenant, property known as 386 Canal S
from
November 20 1992  to        December 31,, 19 92.

Terms of Sublease: The Subtenant agrees to comply with all terms and conditions of the lease entered into by the Tenant, including the prompt payment of all rents. The lease is annexed and its terms are incorporated into this agreement by reference. The Subtenant agrees to pay directly to Landlord the monthly lease rent, and all other rental charges hereinafter due, and otherwise assume, perform and observe all of Tenant's obligations during the sublease period and to fully indemnify Tenant from any liability arising from same.

Security Deposit: The Subtenant agrees to pay to Tenant herewith the sum of 500.00 as a security deposit, to be promptly returned to Subtenant upon the termination of this sublease and upon compliance by Subtenant of all conditions of this sublease.

If lot is properly cleaned by 12/31/92, the deposit will be refunded. (Inventory) Attached to this agreement is an inventory of items or fixtures on the above described property on see below , 19 . The Subtenant agrees to replace or reimburse the Tenant for any missing or damaged items.

Landlord's Consent: The Landlord consents to this sublease and agrees to promptly notify the Tenant at 12 Center St., Springfield, NJ 07081 if the Subtenant fails to make timely rent payments or is in breach of this agreement. Nothing herein shall constitute a release of Tenant who shall remain bound under this lease. Nothing herein shall constitute a consent to any further sublease or Assignment of Lease.

Surrender of Premises: At the expiration of the sublease term, Subtenant shall quit and surrender the premises in as good a condition as they were at the commencement of this sublease, reasonable wear and tear excepted.

Default: If any default is made in the payment of rent, or if there is default in any other provision of either the lease or sublease, then at the option of either Tenant or Landlord, this sublease shall terminate and either Landlord or Tenant may re-enter and retake possession of said premises and either Landlord or Tenant may make claim for any unpaid rent or other damages arising from said breach, provided Tenant may retake possession upon payment of all rent arrearage or other cure of default.

Special Provisions:

1. The electric MUST be transfered from Mobil to DMV Express for the period of this lease (11/20/92 to 12/31/92).
2. The building on the property is to be kept locked at all times. DMV personal do not have permission to enter the building for any reason (other then electrical reasons).
3. Cost of 41 day sublease is $2000. plus a refundable deposit of $500. to be paid on 11/20/92 in the form of a cashiers check or cash only.

IN WITNESS WHEREOF, the parties set their hands and seal this day and year first above written.

DOCUMENT 6

### UNITED STATES DISTRICT COURT
#### PROBATION OFFICE
### DISTRICT OF NEW JERSEY

DAVID A. MASON
F PROBATION OFFICER

CHIEF PROBATION OFFICERS
WILLIAM P. CARROLL
OSEPH J. NAPURANO
ERIC K. SNYDER

July 21, 1993

U.S. COURTHOUSE
50 WALNUT ST.
ROOM 1001
NEWARK, NJ 07101-0459
(201) 645-6161

Mr. Craig Jacob
1282 Wood Valley Road
Mountainside, New Jersey 07092

Dear Mr. Jacob:

On February 15, 1989 you were sentenced on charges of Mail Fraud (3 counts) and Credit Card Fraud (4 counts) in U.S. District Court, Northern District of Illinois. As part of your sentence, you were ordered to pay $350 special assessment and restitution in the amount of $200,009.65. According to the U.S. Probation Office Eastern District of New York, you were released from the custody of the Bureau of Prisons on August 7, 1992. Your five year term of probation commenced on August 7, 1992.

You are scheduled to meet with the undersigned officer on Wednesday, August 4, 1993 at 10:00 a.m. We are located at the following address:

> U.S. Probation Office
> Martin Luther King Federal Courthouse
> 50 Walnut Street - Room 1001
> Newark, New Jersey 07101
> (201) 645-2990

At that time, bring all paperwork, such as official court and other legal documents. In addition, please provide receipt of special assessment and restitution payments which you have made.

Very truly yours,

David A. Mason, Chief
U.S. Probation Officer

Thomas J. Stone
U.S. Probation Officer

TJS:jbm

STEPHEN J. RACKMILL
CHIEF PROBATION OFFICER

EASTERN DISTRICT OF NEW YORK
PROBATION OFFICE

70 CLINTON STREET, ROOM 406
BROOKLYN 11201-4201
718-330-1828

U.S. COURTHOUSE
2 UNIONDALE AVENUE
UNIONDALE, NY 11553-1288
516-463-7140

U.S. COURTHOUSE
300 RABRO DRIVE
HAUPPAUGE 11788
516-682-1108

Brooklyn, New York
November 2, 1993

Mr. Craig Jacob
82-77 116th Street
Queens, New York 11418

RE:  RESTITUTION PAYMENTS

Dear Mr. Jacob:

Please be advised that you will be required to pay $8,200 per month toward your restitution in order to satisfy this court ordered obligation by September 1995.

Additionally, your appointment has been rescheduled. Please report on Wednesday, November 10, 1993, at 10:00 a.m. Provide a certified cashier's check in the amount of $8,200.

If you have any questions, you may contact the undersigned at (718) 330-7246.

Very truly yours,

STEPHEN J. RACKMILL
Chief U.S. Probation Officer

DARCY A. ZAVATSKY
U.S. Probation Officer

DAZ:es

# Violation of Probation Report

NAME:
Craig Barry Jacob

MARITAL STATUS:
Married

ADDRESS:
45 Harrison Ave
Waldwick, N.J. 07463

NUMBER OF DEPENDENTS:
None

AGE:
41

ORIGINAL OFFENSE:
Mail Fraud, Credit Card
Fraud (18 USC 1341),
18 USC 1029(a) (2),
Class C Felonies

DATE OF BIRTH:
February 3, 1953

DEFENSE COUNSEL:
Michael J. Klapper, Esq.
160 Front Street
New York, New York
10038
(212) 248-0848

SEX: Male

CITIZENSHIP: USA

## DOCKET NO.: 94-CR-185

DEPUTY CHIEF,                    U.S. PROBATION
ASSISTANT                       OFFICER:
U.S. ATTORNEY:                  Darcy A. Zavatsky
Keith Krakaur, Esq.


PLEA:    On September 2, 1988, the probationer
         pled guilty to three counts of Mail Fraud
         and four counts of Credit Card Fraud, in
         the Northern District of Illinois.


SENTENCE IMPOSED


DATE OF SENTENCE:    On February 15, 1989


Count 9:   Five years probation, $200,009.65
           restitution, and 1 $50 special assess-
           ment. Following the completion of his
           prison term on September 20, 1990
           (subject sentenced to 32 months
           imprisonment on Counts 1,2,5,6,7&8),
           Jacob began serving time for a previous
           parole violation. He was subsequently
           released via mandatory release on May
           1, 1992, however, his probation
           commenced via inactive status on
           September 20, 1990. On March 7, 1994,
           jurisdiction of this case was trans-
           ferred to the Eastern District of New
           York and assigned to Your Honor.
           Jacob's probation terminates on
           September 15, 1995.

SENTENCING ALTERNATIVES

Your Honor may continue the probationer on probation (without extending the term), modify or enlarge the conditions, or revoke probation and impose a period of incarceration of not more than 10 years as per 18 USC 3565(a).

ORIGINAL OFFENSE:

From June 1987 through May 1988, in the Northern District of Illinois, the defendant devised a scheme and subsequently successfully defrauded various credit card companies of money and property by means of false pretenses. Specifically, Jacob obtained through false representations, names, and personal and financial information about true credit card holders, at least 23 credit cards from various credit card issuing companies. He then represented to these companies, that he was the true card holder and informed that his credit card had been lost or stolen, and provided a change of address which in actuality would be a post office pick up, a private mail receiving service or his home address. Finally, he used these three credit cards in an amount in excess of $200,000, and paid the credit card companies with checks, knowing that there were insufficient funds in the accounts.

Although the original offense occurred in the District of Illinois, Jacob's supervision was immediately transferred to the Eastern District of New York, given his residence in Brooklyn. Due to ongoing criminal investigations by local law enforcement agencies, we requested jurisdiction in this

case. One January 28, 1994, the Honorable Reena
Raggi accepted jurisdiction and effective March 7,
1994, jurisdiction was transferred and assigned to
Your Honor.

SPECIFIC VIOLATIONS OF PROBATION:

The supervisee failed to conform to the following conditions of his probation as set forth on the
form signed by him on May 17, 1993.

### Charge Nos. 1a, 1b, 1c: Check Fraud, Theft by Deception, and Conspiracy

In violation of the mandatory condition prohibiting criminal conduct, the probationer was
arrested on June 1, 1994, by Marlboro and Randolph,
New Jersey Police Departments, and charged with
Check Fraud, Theft by Deception, and Conspiracy. He
committed similar offenses in the Township of
Montgomery, but to date has not been formerly
charged.

### Evidentiary Support:

By way of background, on January 22, 1993, the
probationer entered the New Jersey Automobile Club
(AAA) in Springfield, NJ, and applied for and subsequently received, a basic club membership in the
name of Samuel Zirlin.

On January 23, 1993, Jacob entered the AAA Club
in Randolph, New Jersey, and presented himself as
club member Samuel Zirlin. He presented a Federal
Credit Bank Cashier's check in the amount of
$10,000 bearing the name of Samuel Zirlin. As pro-
cedure would require, the teller called the telephone number (201-945-9666) which appeared on the

check in order to verify the status of the accounts, and the party answering the phone confirmed the validity of the account. It was later revealed by records of New Jersey Bell, that this telephone number is registered to a pay phone located on the New Jersey Turnpike. The probationer then purchased $10,000 worth of American Express Traveler's cheques, which were subsequently cashed at various casinos in Atlantic City, New Jersey, on January 26 and 27, 1993.

On January 25, 1993, between the hours of 11:00 a.m. and 1:30 p.m. in the Townships of Marlboro and Montgomery, New Jersey, AAA offices were entered by the probationer, who represented himself as Samuel Zirlin. At each location, Jacob presented a fraudulent Federal Credit Bank Cashier's check which bore the name of Samuel Zirlin, and were in the amount of $10,000 each. The bank telephone number listed on the check, again went to a pay phone located on the New Jersey Turnpike. Once the tellers placed confirmation calls to "the bank phone number", the checks were later cashed at various locations in Manhattan and New Jersey.

Search warrants served upon Bell Atlantic Mobile and AT&T, revealed that numerous calls were placed from Jacob's cellular phone number, (212) 699-0269, to the pay phone numbers displayed on the counterfeit checks as the number for the banks, on the same dates (January 23 and 25) and during the same exact time periods on which the frauds occurred in all three New Jersey AAA offices. On March 31, 1994, Detective Brian Hall conducted a photo array with the witness in the Marlboro AAA Fraud, "Mrs. Nancy Gordon," in which she positively identified Jacob

as the individual who presented her with the counterfeit check on January 25, 1993. When asked if
she was sure, she replied, "yes, after all, he cost
me my job. When I saw his photograph, my eyes went
right to him." Jacob has also been linked to five
fraudulent Family Savings Society Teller's checks,
each in the amount of $5,000, which were cashed at
a AAA Club in Philadelphia in early March 1993.
Specifically, the telephone number which appeared
on the checks (215) 627-8583, was "call forwarded"
to Jacob's cellular telephone, and called on the
dates during the same time frames in which the
checks were cashed.

On June 1, 1994, the probationer was arrested by
Detective of the Marlboro and Randolph Police
Departments and charged with Check Fraud, Theft by
Deception and Conspiracy. He was additionally
charged with Forgery in the Township of Randolph.
Bail was subsequently set at $50,000 (no 10%), in
both municipalities. On June 3, 1994, Jacob posted
the $1000,000 bail through a bail bondsman and was
subsequently released.

### Charge No. 1d: Forgery

In violation of the mandatory condition prohibiting criminal conduct, the probationer was arrested
on June 1, 1994, by Randolph Township Detective Tom
Copeland, and in addition to the three above noted
charges, he was also charged with Forgery.

### Evidentiary Support:

In addition to the charges outlined in the
"Evidentiary Support" section of Charge 1 (a

through c), the probationer was also charged with
Forgery in the Randolph Township. Specifically, the
probationer fraudulently represented himself as
Samuel Zirlin, and under that name obtained a AAA
Club membership on January 22, 1993. He subsequently presented that card to a teller at the AAA
office in Randolph, NJ, which enabled him to cash
a counterfeit cashier's check in the amount of
$10,000, on January 23, 1993.

### Charge No. 2: Bank Fraud

In violation of the mandatory condition prohibiting criminal conduct, the probationer committed Bank Fraud in Morgantown, West Virginia,
between the dates of November 17, 1993, and January
12, 1994.

### Evidentiary Support:

On November 17, 1993, the probationer entered the
Citizen's Bank of Morgantown located on High Street
in Morgantown, West Virginia, and presented a New
Jersey driver's license in the name of Jose Gomez.
He opened a checking account with an initial
deposit of $200 cash, in that name.

On November 29, 1993, the probationer deposited
a Difeo Leasing check in the amount of $4,900,
which was subsequently returned to the bank stamped
"Account Closed." Between the dates of December 1,
1993 and January 11, 1994, Jacob deposited a total
of six counterfeit checks drawn on the account of
Fairleigh Dickinson University totaling $24,364.59.

It is also noted that during the period which the
account was open, Jacob wrote a total of five

checks. Three of those checks were payable to betting establishments in the respective amounts of
$3,4000, $1,400, and $3,500. The fourth check was
utilized to purchased $8,000 worth of traveler's
checks, and the fifth was used to purchase a bank
check payable to N.Y.R.A., Inc. Additionally, he
made a total of nineteen ATM withdrawals totaling
$3,520, from six different states within a one
month period.

It is noted that Jacob was positively identified
through a color photograph by Ms. Ruth Ann Semel,
the Citizen Bank teller who opened his account in
the alias of Jose Gomez. Additionally, Mark Yost of
Mailboxes Unlimited located at 364 1/2 Patterson
Drive, Morgantown, West Virginia (the address which
Jacob provided to Citizen's Bank as his personal
residence), picked Jacob out of a six photo array
and informed that the probationer had a mailbox at
the above noted location, in the name of Jose
Gomez.

The Bank of New York in Rutherford, New Jersey
suffered a loss of $19,994.33, as a check in the
amount of $4,370 was returned to the Bank of New
York, from Citizen's Bank after Jacob's account was
closed. The undersigned spoke with Lenny Zuzillio
of the Protection Control Department with the Bank
of New York and he advised that they plan to file
federal charges against the probationer.

Charges Nos. 3a, 3b, 3c: Bank Fraud, Check Fraud,
Forgery

In violation of the mandatory condition prohibiting criminal conduct, the probationer entered

One Valley Bank in Morgantown, West Virginia, on November 17, 1993, and opened a checking and savings account in the name of William Grillo. On November 26, 1993, he deposited two fraudulent Metropolitan Life Insurance checks totaling $9,268.10, into that same bank account.

## Evidentiary Support:

By way of background, on November 17, 1993, the probationer, utilizing a fraudulent New Jersey driver's license and operating under the alias of William Grillo, entered One Valley Bank located at 466 High Street in Morgantown, West Virginia and opened a checking and savings account using $1000 cash for the initial deposit. He provided a personal address of 1000 Morgantown Avenue, Fairmont, West Virginia, which is actually a post office pick up.

On November 26, 1993, Jacob, continuing under the guise of William Grillo, entered the bank and deposited two counterfeit Metropolitan Life Insurance checks (#'s 002328745 and 002320343) in the respective amounts of $4,462.20 and $4,805.90. Fortunately, before any substantial loss was suffered by the bank, Met Life advised the bank that the two checks were counterfeit. Philip Erickson, Supervising Auditor in the Fraud Detection and and Investigation Department of Metropolitan Life, reports that two other Met Life checks were cashed in China and Singapore in the amounts of $39,007.81 and $88,610.05, in the name of Ng Hock Soon. It is significant that all four checks had the word Pittsburgh misspelled (Pittsburg) and the same invalid zip code (1523-1350). Moreover, the account numbers on the counterfeit checks are actual account numbers of two of their legitimate account holders, and the counterfeit checks also exhibited legitimate check and block numbers for legitimate checks which had already been issued and cashed through the normal course of business.

Once the bank became aware that the Met Life checks were counterfeit, Jacob's (Grillo) account was frozen. One Valley Bank teller subsequently picked Jacob from a six photo array, and identified him as the individual who falsely represented himself as William Grillo. One Valley Bank only suffered a loss of $100, and therefore, the Morgantown Prosecutor's office will not extradite Jacob for the amount of loss caused to the bank.

## Charge Nos. 4a and 4b: Forgery and Bank Fraud

In violation of the mandatory condition prohibiting criminal conduct, the probationer opened a personal checking account in the name of Arturo Ricci, utilizing a fraudulent New Jersey driver's license and nonresident West Virginia address, on November 27, 1993.

## Evidentiary Support:

On November 27, 1993, the probationer entered the Riverville office of the Huntington Bank in Fairmont, West Virginia, and opened a personal checking account under the alias of Arturo Ricci, utilizing a fraudulent NJ driver license and nonresident West Virginia address. Due to the teller's "suspicions" about Ricci (Jacob), he, Robert Steele, observed Jacob walk to a turquoise, Pontiac Grand Am, yielding New York license plated C58-9AK.

Steele subsequently contacted the police and provided them with the New York plate. It was later
learned that said vehicle was registered to Craig
Jacob. It is noted that the probationer has
informed the Probation Department that said vehicle is owned and driven by him.

On May 18, 1994, Detective Ron Snyder of the
Morgantown Police Department displayed a six photo
array to bank tellers Robert Steel and Debra
Richardson, who opened the account for the probationer on November 27, 1993, at the Riversville,
West Virginia branch. Both tellers picked Jacob
from the array and advised that he had represented
himself as Arturo Ricci. It is also noted that just
days after Jacob opened this particular account and
ordered his checks, he closed the account. Although
the bank has not suffered a loss to date, Jacob
remains in possession of 200 checks for this
account.

## Adjustment to Supervision

Since commencing supervision, the probationer's
employment has been questionable at best, and has
continuously raised our suspicious due to its
nature. Although he is the owner of DMV Express,
Inc. which is designed to assist individuals in
obtaining various Department of Motor Vehicle documents (registrations, titles, etc.) and avoiding
the long lines associated with the DMV, he has used
this corporation to facilitate his criminal behavior. For example, Jacob utilized fraudulent New
Jersey Driver Licenses in order to open bank
accounts under fictitious names, in West Virginia.
Jacob also claims to operate an auction business

through DMV Express, Inc. which is strictly a cash business.

In addition to the charges listed above, on November 18, 1993, the probationer entered the Huntington Bank in Morgantown, West Virginia, and opened a bank account with a $100 cash deposit in the name of Anthony Zito, utilizing a fraudulent New Jersey driver's license. He subsequently deposited a $4,610.10 check from Anheuser Bush Inc., Union, which was made payable to Anthony Zito.

# January 15, 1995

Written from the Metropolitan Detention Center in Brooklyn

Dear Phil,

I will try to make this letter as short as possible. What I am about to write is what happened in my life from the time that I was released from prison in July 1991.

Two weeks after my release from prison to the Philadelphia halfway house I met my now wife Mary for the first time in Atlantic City. My parents were aware that I had been writing to Mary, who is Jamaican, for the past year, and that it appeared that I had fallen in love with her through letters. I continued to see Mary on and off over the months. I mentioned Mary often to my parents, but they never commented until in February 1992 when I asked them to meet Mary. My father agreed to meet her with my mother and a date was set up for a Saturday evening at a restaurant in Somerville, New Jersey. Shortly after the date was set it was quickly cancelled, because my mother claimed that the meeting was not discussed with her, thus she refused to go.

In private my father spoke with her and she then agreed to the meeting.

Very little was said at the dinner. I introduced Mary to my parents and my parents to Mary. My father and Mary did a little talking, my mother did not say a word, she only stared at Mary with a phony smile. The following day, I asked my parents what they thought of Mary, my father commented that she appeared to be a nice person, my mother did not say anything in front of my father. Later that day when my father had left the house, my mother approached me and said, "Your better than that, I met a real nice girl at the United Jersey Bank that wants to go out with you. Please get rid of this other girl." I responded with, "I love Mary, and I'll probably marry her." The conversation ended. The following weekend I spent with my parents and my children, I was still living at the Manhattan halfway house and was permitted to go home on weekends. Again, Mary came up, as did a conversation over money. I was aware that my parents were very wealthy because my mother's father had just recently died and left all his money, stocks, bonds, and his house to my mother and my uncle. During the 3 years that I spent in jail my parents visited me with my children almost every other weekend, we talked about my future and my mother made it clear to me that, if I needed money to go into business when I was released, it would be there waiting for me.

Well I was ready to start my own business. I wanted to become an auctioneer. I would have to rent a building, get licensed, buy a van, buy goods and advertise. I figured that this would cost me somewhere in the neighborhood of $10,000. I told my mother my intentions and for the first time in my life she refused to give me the money, she told me to get it from Mary. I asked her why she had been telling me for years that she would give me what I needed to go into business. She responded by saying, "If you want to go into business in Israel, I will pay for that and we will all move and you will forget about Mary." I refused and said, "I will get the money from Mary if I have to." The conversation ended. The following day my mother told me that if I got rid of Mary that she would buy two homes next to each other and give me one to live in with my children and she would live in the other with my father. (I grew up with my grandparents living next to my parents and my grandfather bought my parents' home.) At that point I told my parents that I was planning to marry Mary and that I would be taking the children back, so that I could raise them with Mary. My father, in a mad voice said, "Your not getting the children back, we have custody." I had given him temporary custody of the children when I went to prison because the children's mother had got involved with drugs and I feared that she might take the children. I told my father that he only had temporary custody. My father responded with, "I will get full custody then."

I was in shock that my parents were not going to give me my children back. I argued with my father, explaining that I planned on buying a home right near them and they would always be able to see the children. He said, "No, you will get the children back when I want to give them back." The following day I called the Jewish Family service in Elizabeth and asked for an appointment. I sat down with a counselor "Sarah Jones" and I explained why I had contacted her, she called my parents and set up an appointment.

A week later we were all at the Jewish Family Service center. I wanted to know why my parents were going to make me fight for my children back and why my mother had refused to give me any money. I had already gotten the money that I needed from Mary, but I wanted to know why she had reneged on her promises. The session started and I asked the first question. I asked, "Why won't you give me back the children?" and my father responded, "Like I told you I will give them back to you when I feel like." I asked, "When will you feel like, what does that exactly mean, does that mean 3 months from now or 5 years from now?" My father responded with, "I don't know, like I said, when I feel like." I turned to Sarah Jones and said, "Would you comment on my father's answer," and she said, "No, I make no comments, I only listen." I then turned to my mother and said, "Why have you cancelled all the credit cards that you gave me when I got out of jail, and closed the bank account that you opened for me?" My mother did not respond. I again turned to Sarah Jones and said, "I thought we were here to resolve problems, ask questions and give answers." Sarah Jones responded, "I am only here to listen." At this point I turned to my parents and said, "I can't believe that you are refusing to give me back my children, if you're going to sit here and tell me that I can't have my children back and then I have to hire an attorney with the money that Mary has ready for a down payment on a house, when I do get the kids I might just take them to San Francisco, why are you doing this to me?" They did not respond, I left the room and drove right to the court house, where I filed the necessary papers for the return of my children, a battle that would take 26 months and cost me $40,000.

For 26 months I was in and out of court. My parents spent in my opinion $150,000 on lawyers, private investigators, and other tactics. DYFAS was called in 5 times, in which my parents filed phony claims that were all dismissed. I constantly had private investigators on my tail, they came to my auctions and snooped around my DMV office. They illegally accessed my TRW credit report. My children carried a cellular phone, that my parents bought them. My son lost his, and my father took my six-year-old son to the police station where I lived to file a complaint against me that I stole the cellular phone, even though my son told my father that he believes he lost it while he was with him. My parents hired a psychiatrist that they used as their hired gun in court. He lied again and again. He had told me, my attorney, the psychiatrist I retained, and my wife that he was going to recommend to the court that I should be given custody of the children.

During the custody battle of 26 months, one of the private investigators hired by my parents contacted the United States Attorneys Office in Chicago, and asked the status of my parole or probation. They were informed that I was terminated in

August of 1992. My parents had all of my court papers as well as my judgement and conviction which had the sentence that I had received in Chicago, which was 32 months in prison and 5 years probation to follow. The probation was to end in 1995, and my parents realized that I had been terminated too early and that there must have been a mistake. Immediately my parents and (or) one of their private investigators called Chicago and demanded that my probation be reinstated.

Shortly after I received a letter from Trevor Reed, my old probation officer, the letter stated,"Please come to my office, your probation has been reinstated, you were released early in error." I met with Mr. Reed and he informed me that my probation was being transferred to Newark since I now live in Union County. A day or so later I received a visit at my home from a Mr. Stone. He had just left my parents' home, and my parents told him that I was a piece of trash, and that anything I told him would be a lie. I had a recording going when he walked into my home. He interviewed Mary and me in the living room. He told me that I was now on his caseload, that he wanted to see me once a week. He told me that I could no longer go to New York where I owned the Auction House and where I earned 75% of my income. He said he could care less about that, he asked me if the state knew that I was the owner of DMV Express and that I had a criminal record, I told him no and he said that I would have to inform them immediately or he would. (I told him that they would close me up if they knew I had a criminal record. He said he could care less.) He told me that

I was to make restitution of at least $1000 per month. I asked him how I could come up with that kind of money, if I can't run my businesses anymore, he said he didn't know and didn't care. He told me to sell the business and my cars and turn the proceeds over to him, which would be applied to restitution. He threatened to violate my probation if I did not follow his orders. He then went on to say that he knows all about me and that I am not a creditable person. Those were the exact words that my father had used in court just a few days earlier. So, I asked him "Did you talk to my parents?" He responded with, "None of your business, I don't answer questions for you, you answer them for me." He told me to report to him the following week.

The following day I called my old Brooklyn parole officer Trevor Reed and I told him what had happened. I explained that this man was completely destroying my life. This was when Trevor Reed told me that my parents were the ones who had my probation reinstated. Trevor Reed explained to me that I was not on Mr. Stone's caseload as of yet, and that all my records were still with him. Trevor Reed told me that if I moved back to the Eastern District of New York, I would not have to deal with Stone and that none of the probation officers in Brooklyn were anything like Stone.

I loved the house that I was living in, I was in the mist of working out a deal to buy the home. It was very convenient. The bus to New York was close, so Mary had no problems getting to work in New York, my DMV office was only 2 miles from the house, and the Auction was only 30 minutes, and on top of that, my children's home was less than 10 blocks. But since I had to move, I went to Staten Island looking for a home, twice I signed leases and both times when they seen that my wife was black they refused to let us move in. Both cases are slated for trial in the near future. I finally found a home in Kew Gardens, the location was not good at all, it took Mary longer to get to work from Kew Gardens than it did from Jersey, and for me it was a horror, fighting the traffic everyday.

As soon as I moved into the new home I met with Trevor Reed and he told me that he would not be my parole officer, but not to worry, I had a good guy. A week later I received a letter to report, and like Trevor Reed said I was assigned to a nice guy, I was in his office for 3 minutes when his phone rang and then he told me that my probation officer had been changed to Darcey Zavatsky.

I met with Darcey Zavatsky a week later after she sent me a letter ordering me to bring a certified check to her for $8000, I brought her a check for $1000 and told her I could in no way afford $8000, she did not comment. She told me to fire any person that worked for either of my businesses that had an arrest record. I explained to her that 5 of my people that worked for me were hired by me at the request of the federal halfway house in New York and they had been with me for over a year, she said she didn't care and ordered me to fire them at once. She ordered me to break up with my partner, she then ordered me to advise the State of New Jersey that I owned DMV Express and that I was a convicted felon. She ordered me to bring her all my tax papers from day one, cancelled checks from the business, and personal, telephone bill personal and business, cellular phone bills, and copies of all employment applications. She ordered me never to bring a tape recorder in her office, like I had done to Stone. She knew why I relocated, she had spoke to my parents and Stone. She did not appear to be worse then Stone because she agreed to let me travel wherever I had to for business.

I believe that behind my back she was in constant contact with my parents, the judge on the custody case and my parents' private investigators. So many things she would say during my visits with her clearly told me that.

For the first 5 months I gave her $1000 each month and then I told her that because of her, I was no longer making the kind of money that I was making before, because I no longer had my partner and I had to hire unexperienced people, since she made me fire all of my best workers. She told me to take a loan on my life insurance policy and turn the money over to her. I argued that I wanted to save money in the bank for an emergency or at least pay my taxes in April, she replied with, "No, you will hold nothing in the bank and you can worry about your taxes when the time to pay it comes."

Darcey Zavatsky knew that I was a workaholic, but would never admit it. I always was able to tell her what I had done yesterday, what I was doing today and what I had planned for the following week. She visited my office in Springfield a number of times, she came to my home 3 times that I know about, and she attended at least one auction, though I invited her to several.

It was February, I believe, that Darcey asked me to stand up against the wall while she took about eight photos of me. I asked what this was all about and she said, "You have been a busy, busy man Mr. Jacob. By the way are you with the children every Saturday?" I responded with, "I have never missed a visit in my entire life," meaning I was with the children every single Saturday. She then said, "Don't you sometimes drop them places on Saturdays?" and I said, "No, unless it's for 15 minutes to run to the store for chicken or pizza." I had no idea why she would ask such a question, I would later find out.

In early 1994 business was slow, I no longer had the cash flow that I had with my partner, because Ms. Zavatsky made us break up. I had to pass up good auction buys, I had run up a lot of debts, due to the custody case. I paid my custody attorney $20,000, I paid an expert witness between $7500 and $10,000, I paid the hired gun psychiatrist thousands, I paid thousand for depositions, I lost thousands due to my moving expenses. I also made some bad auction deals that cost me plenty. I paid another 2 attorneys $10,000 to handle other legal matters, I spent $3,000 on transcript for my custody appeal. I paid the probation dept. about $6500.

In May of 1994 I filed bankruptcy in Brooklyn Federal Court. None of the creditors complained, though Ms. Zavatsky objected and claimed that the filing was fraudulent, without explanation. My bankruptcy was still pending when I was remanded on December 1, 1994.

In late May 1994, I received a call from my probation officer, she told me to be at home at 10 am on June 1, 1994, because she was making a house visit. I had an auction buy to make on that day, which was scheduled for 1 pm. I had made arrangements with my driver to meet me at my home at 11 am, so that we could go up to Westchester together to make the buy.

At 10 am my probation officer was at my house with 2 detectives, one detective was from Morris County, New Jersey, the other was from Monmouth County, New Jersey. They immediately told me that I was under arrest for passing bad checks. They made me walk around the house with the probation officer, while the probation officer observed whatever I had in my home with the detectives. They then led me outside where my probation officer searched my van, questioning the items that were in the van. I then was led back into my home. At that moment my driver "George Fenton" arrived, he entered the house and was handcuffed. He drove up in my Grand Am, he had been using that car while I was driving another car and the van. The probation officer immediately asked him what he was doing driving my blue Grand Am, and he replied, "I drive whatever car Jake tells me I can drive."

Both George and I were brought to the Waldwick police dept. One of the detectives told George they believed that he had printed the counterfeit checks that I used in the crime. George claimed that he knew nothing about nothing. The detective gave George his card and told him that he better remember quick, because he'd be coming back to get him soon.

The Waldwick police permitted me to call an attorney, while my probation officer and one of the detectives listened on another line. I called the attorney and began to speak, when I could hear breathing on the line, I yelled out that I wanted to know if I could make a private call, and the Waldwick police came into the office that I was in and yelled, "You have a private line, you fuckin' wiseguy." I had no private line, but all I really wanted to do was to let the attorney know what happened and where I was going.

The detectives sat down with me in the office and told me that they knew that I committed the crimes, but that they were willing to drop the charges if I plead guilty to probation violation, thus they said I would go back to federal prison. I told them I was innocent, knew nothing about these charges, and would make no deals. I was put into the police car by Marlboro Detective Hall, who told me that I was a piece of shit on the way to the jail and he expressed how he hated people like me.

That evening I was placed in the Monmouth County jail. The following day I saw pre-trial services, they took all the information from me regarding community ties, employment, family status. After the interview they advised me that I would most likely be released on my own recognizance (no bail). That afternoon I saw the judge in Monmouth County. My bail was set at $100,000 cash only, the stated that he had just received a fax from Ms. Zavatsky and that was the reason for the outrageous bail. He did not say in court exactly what the fax said, other then I was immediately being violated on probation.

The following day my wife met with a bondsman in Asbury Park where she paid a $10,000 fee to have the $100,000 posted and I was released. The following week I again saw Ms. Zavatsky, at which time she advised me that I was being violated immediately for the crime that I committed, I argued that I committed no crime and she didn't respond. The following week I drove to Freehold where the Monmouth County Courthouse was located and requested the discovery items on the case and finally I saw how I was tied into this Counterfeit Check Fraud Scheme. A cellular phone owned by DMV Express was used to call a pay phone on the parkway, which was tied into the crime.

I was not involved in this crime, but it was certainly possible that I did call that parkway number, if someone had beeped me from it, but that was two years ago, and I couldn't remember if I made the call to the pay phone or if my partner at the time, Ron Foster, made the call. Ron had the phone more than I did, so I assumed that it was him.

I knew that I had not committed the crime, but I was curious to know if Ron had anything to do with it. I knew Ron had moved to South America, and I tried to contact him but couldn't locate him. The crime was sort of similar to something that I done in the past and it was most likely done by someone who read my book.

I was willing to go all the way, no way would I plead guilty to a crime I did not commit, or knew

nothing about. When I received my Violation of
Probation notice I hired an attorney to represent
me named Robert Blossner. In July 1994, I appeared
before Judge Trager for the violation hearing, at
which time I found out that I was being violated
for at least 10 crimes that I did not commit. The
probation officer asked to have me remanded on the
grounds that I was a danger to society and that I
committed all the crimes listed in her report.
Judge Trager stated he needed some sort of evidence to look at, before he would remand me. A new
hearing date was set for late August, the probation dept. cancelled that date and another one was
set for late October, the probation dept. canceled
that date again, then on December 1, 1994 I
appeared in court for the new hearing. As soon as
I walked into the courtroom with my attorney, the
asst. US attorney handed my atty. new discovery.
At this point a postponement was in order, my
atty. did not request one. The probation officer
took the stand and said that Mr. Jacob was positively identified by 3 banks in West Virginia as
the person who entered their bank a year ago and
opened phony acct's. This was a Saturday, and that
was totally impossible because I was with my children, (now I knew why the PO had questioned me
about dropping the children). Then the detective
from Monmouth County took the stand and he said
that I was positively identified by a Nancy Gordon
as the person who passed a bad cashiers check at
the AAA office 2 years ago. The judge ordered me
remanded and set a sentencing date for 10 days
away. I asked the judge if I were to go to court
in New Jersey and found not guilty would he bring

me back before him and release me. The asst. DA
jumped in and said "Your Honor, you have already
found Mr. Jacob guilty by preponderance of the
evidence, even if they find him not guilty at a
trial, you can still keep the sentence that you
give him." The judge replied, "I don't feel that
would be fair, I couldn't do that."

The following day I made up my mind to subpoena
every single person who either ID'ed me or who was
the person who allegedly accepted a counterfeit
check from me, I was also going to subpoena all the
bank officers in West Virginia who allegedly opened
these phony bank accounts for the suspect.

The person who later identified me from an array
gave a totally different description when she was
first questioned. She was also read her Miranda
rights, which made it clear that she was a suspect.
I believed that she had made an honest mistake when
she later picked me out of the array with the help
of Detective Hall. The discovery material that I
received contained pictures of a suspect who only
slightly resembled me. I asked my wife to go to her
home and show her a picture of the person I suspected of committing these crimes all over
Pennsylvania and New Jersey. If she could ID him,
I would be cleared. When my wife got to her home and
identified herself, Nancy Gordon refused to look at
any pictures and called the police.

Nancy Gordon was subpoenaed, as were seven other
people 3 from West Virginia Banks and 4 from AAA
offices in New Jersey. On the hearing day the first
person to take the stand was Mr. Steele, Vice Pres.
of Huntington Bank in West Virginia. He was asked

if he had picked my picture out of an array and he said yes. Then he was asked if he sees the person in court who committed the crime (the crime was opening a phony bank account, it turned out that the fool who opened the account made no money off the scam and the bank made a $3800 profit). Mr. Steele stared at me for 10 minutes and then I stood up and said, "Here I am can you see me better now?" Then Steele stated that he could not say that I was the person who opened the bank account a year ago. Next was Debra Richardson who was asked if she had ID'ed me from an array, she was also from the same bank as Steele, and she said that she did. Then she was asked if she saw the person in the courtroom who committed the crime and she looked at me and said, "No." Next was Ruth Ann Semel of Citizens Bank, she was asked if she ID'ed me from an array and she said yes, when asked if she saw the person in the courtroom who committed the crime she said, "No, definitely not." Next came Nancy Gordon of the AAA in Marlboro, New Jersey. She was asked if she was able to identify the person who committed the crime from the array given her a year ago and she said "yes, I could never forget the face, I lost my job because of that person." Then my attorney asked her if she saw the person in the courtroom and she said yes, and pointed to me. I jumped up and said, "Me?" Nancy Gordon replied "I think so." Then my lawyer took the array over to Nancy Gordon, this was the array where she stated that she would never forget the person who committed the crime. Nancy Gordon stared at the array for 5 minutes and then turned to my atty. and said, "I don't remember which one I picked." Then my atty. brought up the fact that she had just stated that the person who committed the crime was approximately 39 years old, (my exact age at the time of the crime). My lawyer brought to her attention that immediately after the crime she told the detectives that the person was in his late 50's. She was showed her statement from 2 years ago and spent 10 minutes reading it, she had forgotten what she had said. It was obvious that she was lying at the request of the detective that was working with my PO in order to violate me. The judge saw how nervous this witness was and refused to permit my atty. from asking her more questions.

Next Linda Smith took the stand. She was from the Montgomery AAA. She stated on the stand that I was positively not the person who committed the crime.

Next Mary took the stand, (my wife) she was asked if I had been with the children and her every Saturday for the last 2 years, and I had been because those were my visiting days, she stated that I never missed a visiting day and I always picked the children up and dropped them off myself. Therefore I could not have been in West Virginia on a Saturday. The judge stated that she couldn't possibly remember if I missed a Saturday visit or not and stated that he couldn't accept that I never missed a visit, and that Mary was just trying to help her husband.

She was also asked if she knew my whereabouts on the 18th of November 1993 and she handed the judge transcripts that showed that on that day the custody trial was taking place in Union County regarding my children, the DA argued that even though it is clear that a hearing took place all day, I might not have showed up for my own trial.

Next Tracey (DMV Secretary) took the stand. There was a 1993 Grand Am involved in one of the crimes, the crime where the criminal lost $3800. This car was registered to DMV, Tracey explained to the court that DMV owned 8 vehicles at the time of the crime and that many of the employees drove the Grand Am, as well as the other autos. She was asked about the cellular phones and she explained that many of the employees used the phones and I used it the least. Then she showed the judge a check that was cashed by me at Statewide Savings in Elizabeth, NJ at 4:30 pm, Nov. 17, 1993, at this time I was suppose to be at a bank in West Virginia, the judge looked at the check and said he may of sent someone to the bank to cash this $1000 check, because he stated that he sent people to the bank to cash his check a lot and thus that does not prove that he was not in West Virginia.

Next I took the stand. I showed the judge a calling card bill which showed that I was in New York, when I was suppose to be in West Virginia, but the judge did not accept that, even though the calls that were made on the card were calls that I made.

After I testified, the judge said "Guilty, I will sentence him next week." I asked the judge if I could hire a handwriting expert to prove my innocence. The judge then stated:"If the handwriting expert says it was you, I will sentence you to 10 years, is that OK?" I said,"Yes most definitely." The judge then replied,"OK I want the government to supply the expert." The govt. then jumped up and said, "Your Honor this is a waste of time. The evidence is overwhelming, this is the last hope of a desperate man, I feel this should not be allowed." The judge then said, "OK, I won't allow it, sentencing next week." (Govt. knew I did not commit these crimes and that they had nothing.)

I hired an expert anyway and then on the day of sentencing my atty. appealed to the judge to set another hearing before sentencing to have the handwriting expert testify. The judge was agreeable, then the govt. complained that the evidence was overwhelming (nonsense) and that they objected. The judge then asked me if I had anything to say, I asked the judge if I said anything could it possibly help me and he said no, not really. Then he said, "I wish you would have said what I wanted to hear," I then asked the judge if he wanted me to say, I was sorry for committing a crime that I did not commit. He did not respond. Then he sentenced me to 7 1/2 years. He said the sentence was for the 2 West Virginia Crimes and the AAA crimes. He was suppose to sentence me for the probation violation, a sentence which by the guidelines carried a sentence of 18-24 months. He stated that he has never went over the guidelines before, he always goes under but I deserve it.

I believe that my parents wrote him a letter asking the judge to put me away for as long as possible, they worked with the PO and other people who had influence, that is why I got this outrageous sentence. I do believe that I will get out earlier via a rule 35. If that fails, I believe I will be granted a new hearing late this year. I typed this letter in a hurry and it's a little messy, I will call you Sunday to make sure you recd it and answer any questions that you may have for me.

Sincerely,
Craig

# About the Author

Phil Berger is one of the country's most noted sports writers. Both his *Miracle on 33rd Street: The New York Knickerbockers' Championship Season* and *Blood Season: Tyson and the World of Boxing* have become classics of the genre. Berger's other book credits include: *The Last Laugh: The World of the Standup Comic, Punch Lines: Berger on Boxing* and two novels, *Big Time*, which is loosely based on rogue basketball star Jack Molinas, and *Deadly Kisses*, a mystery set in 1930s Hollywood. A former boxing correspondent for *The New York Times*, Berger's award-winning work regularly appears in the pages of a variety of publications, including *The New York Times Sunday Magazine, Playboy, Esquire, The Village Voice, Penthouse, Sport, Inside Sports* and *The Washington Post*.